GINNY CRACKFART

LOUISE MCGOW

Greenstream Publishing

Greenstream Publishing
12 Poplar Grove
Ryton on Dunsmore
Warwickshire
CV8 3QE

www.GreenstreamPublishing.com
First Edition
Published by Greenstream Publishing, October 2012.

Copyright © Louise McGow 2012.

Louise McGow asserts the moral right to be identified as the author of this work.

ISBN 978-1-907670-26-8

A catalogue record for this book is available from the British Library.

All rights reserved. No part of this publication may be reproduced, stored in a retrieval system, or transmitted, in any form or by any means, electronic, mechanical, photocopying, recording or otherwise, without the prior permission of the author.

Contents

Chapter One 1

Chapter Two 8

Chapter Three 17

Chapter Four 24

Chapter Five 34

Chapter Six 42

Chapter Seven 50

Chapter Eight 53

Chapter Nine 63

Chapter Ten 72

Chapter Eleven 78

Chapter Twelve 89

Epilogue 97

Chapter One

Friday, February 24th 1996. The council phoned, offering me a flat to rent.

At last, freedom! I desperately needed to flee my parents home, the family home in which I had lived for almost thirty years. Not that my folks were the problem, in fact nobody could have wished for more loving and supportive parents. It was the ever present, over bearing, character lynching, paranoid schizophrenic neighbour from hell that was driving me out.

Until 1992 I had been content living at home being fed, watered and groomed even, like a chick too comfortable and afraid to leave the nest. It suited my lifestyle. I was in a good job, earning an average wage that supported my active and extremely hectic social life. I really didn't have time to play at housekeeping, not that I really wanted to anyway...at least I thought I didn't.

It was at this time that Ginny Crackfart, as she came to be known because of her inappropriate verbal outbursts, changed from a hermit like creature of habit, into the resident neighbourhood maniac! Of course this behaviour was purely of her own making, as far as we could tell there had never been any dispute between the neighbours, ourselves and Ginny. Her changed behaviour came suddenly like a bolt from the blue.

Ginny had always been a bit of a loner, never wanting to sociable and rarely managing to string a sentence together in conversation. Yet at the same time she had this amazing knack of nosily barking personal questions at you in such a manner, that you found yourself replying. Most of the neighbours being friendly and accepting took her for what she was and got on with their own lives. Nobody was initially nasty to Ginny, but over the years to come this gradually changed and a deep hatred grew, mainly through the fear she left in her trail. A trail which was to change the lives of many, with shocking and devastating results.

We had always thought Ginny was a little strange from the day she had first moved in, some six years earlier, but nobody could actually work out what it was about her that made her appear so odd.

Mum, Dad, my younger sister Karen and myself had been away in Cornwall at the time of Ginny's arrival, but I had returned early much to the surprise of our new neighbour. She had instantly questioned just who exactly was I, where had I been and where was everybody else who lived in 'that' house with me. She was jerking her head and waving her arms in the direction of our house, agitated almost that I wasn't answering quick enough. She had obviously got information from somewhere...perhaps the neighbours, as she seemed to know a great deal about us all anyway, and proceeded to tell me so. I remember thinking, why is she asking if she already knows, how stupid.

I had come home from holiday early because I was unwell but didn't tell her this. The journey back from Cornwall to Reading had really taken its toll on me and standing there in the full glare of the June heat I was beginning to feel worse again. I needed to get indoors to bed, yet I didn't want to appear rude so I let Ginny waffle on for a while longer before managing to cut her off full flow and say, "Oh no, no, you must have been misinformed. This is a kids' home for children with long term behavioural problems. They are away on assessment right now, but you'll soon know when they are back"

Ginny's face registered shock, she went a pale shade of grey and stood there motionless, mouth agape staring at me in utter disbelief, before turning beetroot red, stuttering like a clockwork fish and once again beginning the animated arm waving of earlier. I was desperately trying not to laugh and give the game away. I wasn't being nasty, it was just my silly sense of humour coming out and I hadn't been able to resist the wind up. I picked up my luggage and swiftly moved to unlock the back door while continuing "Well, it was nice meeting you, I hope you settle in okay, I am sure the kids will be excited to have a new neighbour about the place, they do so love a challenge."

On that note I fell through the kitchen door a giggling mass of jelly. Obviously at the time I could not have been aware of Ginny's past mental health problems and to be honest I don't think I had expected such an outburst. Who knows but maybe she was harbouring a grudge that festered away inside her mind all those years, before finally exploding into a torrent of passionate victimisation, that would not only affect myself and my family but anybody who dared to walk past the gates to her house.

We didn't really see much of Ginny or her husband Rob to begin with. To this day I can't recall what Rob looked like. Apparently they worked in the city. We would see the pair of them setting off for London each morning. Rob in his pinned stripe suit and waistcoat, swinging an umbrella that he methodically jabbed the pavement with, and Ginny, hair immaculate and draped in full length heavy blue coat – whatever the weather. Occasionally at weekends we would see the two of them out in the garden. Ginny would be barking orders that the grass was to be precision cut and that the borders were not to be left with a single strand poking out of place. Sometimes if Mum was hanging out the washing, she would stop and have a natter with them over the fence. On one occasion I recall them having a cup of tea together, but Ginny didn't want to come around to ours and sit in the Garden...she stayed firmly rooted on her side of the fence while sipping her tea. It was about an hour later that she obviously felt the need to repay this gesture of neighbourliness and insisted that Mum join them over at their house. It was just so bizarre.

The summer passed quickly and it was early one September morning that my Dad, Bill, noticed that Ginny and Robs' car had been wrecked. The upholstery was raggedly torn to shreds and was hanging from the doors, seats and roof of the car. The dashboard had been smashed leaving a bare mass of limply intertwined wires. It was all very odd, the car had hardly moved from their driveway the whole three or so months that the couple had lived there, yet nobody had seen or heard anything.

It was also about this time that Rob seemed to have disappeared, vanished into thin air. Because of Ginny's behaviour some years later, we were all convinced that she had murdered him and kept his body buried in the garage, or was at least holding him hostage there. This was because she seemed to become obsessed with her crumbling rotten garage and would visit it two or three times a day, like she was checking up on something. There was more than one occasion when Karen and I risked life and limb trying to peak through the now blacked out garage windows, hoping to solve the mystery of the missing Rob! Although Ginny was very secretive about her life, she did make a point of telling Mum and I that Rob was in fact away in Saudi Arabia. Needless to say he never returned that Christmas like she had said he would, and to this day never had. Perhaps he had left her plain and simple and we would never know.

Over the following five to six months we began to notice a change in Ginny. She was even less communicative about herself than ever before, yet extremely, almost to the point of being intrusive, nosy about the lives of everybody else. Not just my family, but the whole street. If you tried to ask her something, perhaps how she was, she would answer by asking a question herself. It was unbelievably frustrating at times. I think we all assumed that in some perverted way Ginny had a problem with the way other people lived their lives. We tried not to judge her and just let her be herself, while continuing to be as friendly as she would allow us.

Sometimes months would pass without sight or sound of her. Of course there were times when we would sit around and talk about Ginny, that is just human nature and in our street neighbours actually cared about each other and worried if things did not appear normal. Nobody could tell if she was ill as she never answered the door so we all just let her have her privacy. Then there she was large as life asking so many damn questions. It was as if she had honed in on our thoughts by some form of telepathic communication, drawing attention away from herself by once again taking an interest in others. So the chatter would die away and life continued as normal...well normal for the rest of us maybe, but I was beginning to realise that perhaps there was something mentally askew with Ginny.

What got me started with this process of thinking was a scene I witnessed between Ginny and her beloved dustbin. It was one of those cold, wintry and overcast afternoons when there wasn't much to do except mope around unmotivated by the impending darkness. I sat watching the rain slam into my bedroom window, each drop a powerful force that once it had found its destination, slowly trickled then died away. I was dying away, it was boring, so frustratingly boring that it must have been a Sunday.

As I sat there just thinking I noticed Ginny come out of her kitchen door and amble into her back garden, almost without purpose. It was sometime before she reappeared lugging her dustbin behind her. Absent minded, I watched as she inspected it top to bottom, twirling it round and around, lifting it up high before finally setting it to rest in the middle of the driveway. For a while Ginny just stood there, but something must have caught her eye as she peered closer, then closer still until the entire upper half of her body was inside the empty bin. I had this urge to flip her legs over and quickly but neatly replace the lid, finishing the job in hand. The idea made me laugh and lifted my spirits, so much so that I picked up the nearest thing – a pair of knickers (clean I must add) and began to dust my room. In the back of my mind though there was something not quite right about this whole incident, but I just couldn't put my finger on just what it was. I went back to the window for another look, I didn't recall seeing Ginny with a cloth or anything but maybe she was just giving the bin a clean out and I simply hadn't noticed. Then it hit me. The entire time this charade had continued, Ginny was out there in the thundering rain, but unlike most people she hadn't had the sense to put on a raincoat. Instead there she was for all to see in her dressing gown and slippers. She was by now soaked to the skin, her quilted gown a sodden rag so heavy that it scraped the floor as she moved. I shivered. It was as if I was feeling the icy rain against my own flesh, on her behalf. I turned away shaking my head in disbelief, who in their right mind would do such a strange thing? I suppose we all do odd things at times and usually in our own minds there is a very good reason why. So I left the room returning Ginny to her privacy.

At first I never told anybody what I had seen, there wasn't really much point as her behaviour soon lapsed into insignificance. It was only when other similarly disturbing events took place, some of which other people had witnessed, did I spill the beans. It seemed everybody in the street had a story to tell about Ginny Crackfart. Behind closed doors we would sit, coffee in hand and have a good laugh at her expense. It didn't mean we all disliked her; I don't think anyone had been able to get close enough to actually like or dislike this mysterious woman. She had never allowed us this privilege. Maybe we were all simply ignorant, blind perhaps to the ins and outs of mental illness and her past history with it. Ginny was simply Ginny!

Towards the end of 1991, Ginny seemed to have retreated indoors completely. There were no more one sided conversations full of personal questions. Occasionally she would be seen at the shopping centre, but would scuttle off in the opposite direction with her head bent low, avoiding anyone from the road as they approached. The garden that was so neatly tended to was left to grow straggly for long periods of time. Now and then Ginny would have bursts of activity, frantically clearing her backlog of jobs. We had worked this out to be when she usually had a visitor coming, and only then. It was like she needed to portray a good clean sane image in a bid to fool people that she was indeed functioning to societies' level of acceptance when in fact nothing could have been further from the truth.

It was on one such occasion that a friend and I watched her drop to her knees and pick ferociously at her concrete driveway. As Ginny had been gardening we just assumed that she was tackling the weeds from between the cracks in it. It took a while for my brain to register that the tool she was using was not that of the gardening type, but a toothbrush! Jo and I went indoors and as curiosity got the better of us we watched from behind the kitchen window. Ginny would pace around for a while before once again dropping to the ground and scrubbing the cold hard concrete in fast circular movements. Concentrating hard with a face set in stone, she bent lower, and lower still until her nose was almost touching the dusty floor. Being so low meant we could no longer see her face clearly, but my imagination could. It would be one of intense confusion, screwed up, cross eyed and dazed like a cartoon character who'd taken a bang to the head. We waited for Ginny to collapse in a defeated heap, cracking jokes as we did so, but that was obviously not in her nature. She would begin her ritual again and again, going back over patches that in my mind had been sanded top perfection. Jo had made her escape while Ginny had been engrossed in the task at hand, but it must have been a good two hours plus, that Ginny had been out there. At least it wasn't raining this time!

Thank heavens for net curtains. I wouldn't have wanted Ginny to know I had been watching the matinee she had been performing. I am not usually the nosy neighbour type but when it came to this woman I was simply transfixed by her bizarre actions. It was of no consequence to me what she did, I simply wanted to know what made her tick, what made her behave in the odd ways that she had been lately. I suppose I am the sort of person that likes to study people, one that would sit at the back of the bus and watch the other passengers, how they sat, how they smoked, comparing the differences while watching for the mounting frustration of an impending traffic jam. I am bit like a curious child who needs to dismantle a mechanical object in the search for understanding.

Chapter Two

I was just eighteen months old when my parents decided to move from Slough, Buckinghamshire as it was then, to Woodley in Berkshire. This rapidly growing estate on the outskirts of Reading was a popular place for the newly married hoping to start a family.

I loved the house that we lived in. I suppose being so young when we had moved here I had no memory of ever living in Slough and could never imagine living elsewhere. In childhood this house had become my home. There was always an affectionate reception from my parents, impregnable by all means, a safe place to run back to after a day of mischievous misadventure. While in adulthood it had become my refuge, a quiet place to retreat to and reflect. This house and the people in it represented an anchor of love and security no matter what the outside world threw at me.

I used to love turning into our road with its neat line of red bricked semi-detached houses, each one with fenced off gardens and driveways. A low brick wall separated most lawns from the pavement, and in summer every house had some sort of blossom tree or a garden heaped high with colourful flowering bushes. I suppose it was a typical estate of suburban sixties, and in my childlike imagination one that would never change. Just how wrong could I be!

Dads' favourite place was his shed. He had built it back in those early days, strategically placed just a whisker from our back door, it still stands weathered and beaten from the changing seasons.

"Solid with years of life left in it", according to Dad. Basically I believe it is only the amount of junk he keeps in it that holds it altogether. This rambling rotten hut is like a musty old antique shop, crammed full of useless relics from the past. Still Dad loves it and that is all that matters.

He usually manages to disappear in to its depths just as dinner is being served and doesn't reappear until we are either serving up pudding or beginning the washing up. It is his place to be alone and to think and take time out of his humdrum life. That said, Dad doesn't have any sense of time.

It was one of those days in March 92 that Ginny Crackfart made her first attempt at sabotaging the peaceful lives we led. Dad was standing in the shed doorway when Ginny for no apparent reason flew out of her door, and like a demon possessed begun to hurl vulgar verbal abuse at him. Shocked he stood stock still not knowing what on heavens earth was happening, while she got louder and nearer until she quite simply grabbed him by the throat and pinned him up against the wall.

Dad is a good man, not the sort of person that could possibly offend anyone, even when provoked he would rather walk away than retaliate.' Docile and harmless, reliable in an emergency, good old Bill' that's what people said. But this doesn't mean he is a push over, in fact Dad is very good with words and will, when necessary, cleverly box his way out of a corner verbally and calmly.

I had never really seen or heard of him losing his temper with anyone, apart from when he'd chase my sister and I up the stairs after we had driven him to despair with our antics as kids. Even then he never lashed out, it was just scare tactics and we knew it. He would corner us in our bedroom and try to give us a stern talking to. We usually had to do our best not to laugh at his seriously stern face. All the same we had great respect for him.

By now Ginny was in full flow, her verbal abuse reducing to a low taunt, "Weak old Bill, married to fat Pat, couldn't do any better, feeble pathetic man"

This would be followed by another torrent of excessively loud foul mouthed swearing. This continued for a few moments before Dad finally leapt into action. Pushing her aside his grasshopper legs carried his tall lean frame over the three foot wire fence separating the two drives. Then giving her a succession of rapid little shoves, he knocked Ginny backwards in the direction of the door she had so belligerently come out of earlier. Over the top of her protesting ranting he bellowed "Get back in your rabbit hutch and sort yourself out".

One last shove sent her flying through the open door, knocking her thick roundish glasses off in the process. I had never seen Dad looking so fierce, he was hopping mad and shaking from head to toe.

Needless to say this was not the end of the matter. While we had all been discussing this peculiar outburst, Ginny had gone inside, dialled 999 for the police and alleged that Dad had just seriously assaulted her. Of course she had forgotten to mention that she had tried to strangle him first. I think Dad was quite relieved to see a police car draw up outside the house a short while later. After the incident he didn't know what to do and being the placid chap he is, I think he not only shocked Ginny by his actions, but he had scared himself too with his overzealous response.

His relief was short lived as heart in mouth we all watched as two officers headed straight for Ginny's beckoning front door. They were privileged; she didn't normally open this to anybody. We all waited in nerve jangling suspense for the policemen to come into us. When they did finally emerge looking a little worse for wear, Dad gabbled some apology for them being called to such a trivial matter. He said it was all very daft. I didn't think it was daft, this mad crazed lunatic witch near on strangled him for no reason. One of the officers laid out the allegations made against him by Ginny and his apologies soon turned sour. She had seriously fabricated the story, making herself totally blameless and Dad the villain. Damn cheek was all he could choke out. I think at this point we were all waiting for Dad to be read his rights and carted off to the police cells. It didn't come to that though as Dad's honesty won the day convincingly and not lying about his response to Ginny's initial attack had won the day.

"Mrs Crackfart is a very strange woman who certainly doesn't have all her marbles about her, don't worry about it. We'll leave it at that." And on that note they left.

A week or so passed and the incident began to fade from all of our minds. The chatter reverted back to everyday life and as nothing else occurred on the Ginny front, we all assumed she had just had a funny half hour.

For the next few months things went from bad to worse. It was only now as her behaviour deteriorated drastically did people begin to realise that perhaps she wasn't simply mad, but suffering some form of mental illness. A subject few people were comfortable with or inclined to know about, while others were totally ignorant. Unless you personally know someone who is or has suffered in this way, I believe you never really take an interest into understanding such a complicated issue.

  I had some years earlier, spent a lot of time befriending patients at a local psychiatric hospital. I can't say I now know or really understand these matters extensively, but I had learned enough to know when a certain behaviour is neither normal or acceptable in today's society, and Ginny's had become just that, unacceptable. Her verbal abuse became a daily ritual. A constant barrage of shouted obscenities met every member of my family as we entered or left the house. What time of day it was of no consequence to Ginny, in her mind all the better if she disturbed the whole street. She seemed to become obsessed, watching our every move from behind her dirty looking curtains. Sometimes though she never even tried to hide the fact she was indeed lying in wait. From the waist up her frame would appear, suddenly filling the empty window as she yanked back the nets and glared out. If this happened I had worked out I had approximately five seconds to get from the front gate, around the side of the house, park my motorcycle and get in through the kitchen door before Crackfart would fly out like a hungry lion unleashed. It became a bit of a competition for all involved, who could run the gauntlet and have the last laugh. Who would come out champion of the day?

  I could manage a ten hour shift at the office, working to tight deadlines and still come away feeling as fresh as a daisy, but those last few yards along the driveway were exhausting. I no longer looked forward to turning into my road with its familiar feeling of security. Instead the tension would begin to creep into my shoulders and Ginny's image would repeatedly enter my mind. She was like a jingle to an advertisement, once heard, never forgotten.

As time went by and our powers of ignoring her were beginning to wind Ginny up, she introduced new tactics to this bizarre game. Along with the obscenities came the face pulling. It certainly was a way of catching our attention. Sticking her tongue out, then putting her thumbs to her temples she would wiggle her fingers about while chanting "nah-nah-nah-nah-nah", just like an irritating five year old. Just as suddenly this childlike behaviour would stop and a threatening, fist waving string of name calling would begin. Apparently I was mad!

"You're mentally ill you are Louise, you listening to me, you're ill, sick. Sad pathetic lunatics like you should be locked up. You poor skinny child, reject of the family, the black sheep, you are a mistake. You don't belong here and I'll get you sorted, you see if I don't."

And so it went on. My Mum was fat Pat, my sister, also a large girl was a prostitute and a no good waster. Ginny never mentioned my older brother Neil though. The only time we ever saw any peace was when he visited, and that wasn't often. This also caused some tension between Neil and myself because he never witnessed any of her mad behaviour and tended to make light of the situation, often implying that I was making a mountain out of a mole hill. Maybe because Neil was six and a half foot and heavily built, Ginny must have realised that even she wasn't a match for him. Then again it could have been tactical on her part, who knows how her mind worked.

Ignoring Ginny was beginning to get difficult, after all there is only so much patience a person can hold out on, and mine was wearing thin, very thin. The abuse had become continuous. It no longer mattered whether we were inside or outside of the house her ranting would go on for hours. Above the washing machine, louder than the television, all you could hear was her grating voice. It cut right through you, not neatly sliced, but jaggedly cut, tearing and ripping you apart. It vibrated on every fibre of your being. I really, really wanted to hit her, and hard. It was frightening how intense that feeling was. If I lost my temper then I knew not only would be as bad as her, but I simply wouldn't stop until Crackfart was pulped!

By the summer of 92 we were unable to even move around the house without her yelling to the whole street, where we were, what we were doing and she certainly made it clear just who she was talking, or should I say, yelling about. "Pat O' Down, Pat O' Down, Pat O' Down you fat old cow, I know you're in there, in the kitchen, I can see I'm watching you". This was a favourite of Ginny's and she always sang it to the tune of 'My darling Clementine'.

One day I was in the bathroom, doing the things you do before taking a shower, when this nah-nah voice wafted in through the barely open window.

"I know what you're doing, I know where you are, I know what you're doing".

Over and over again she repeated this. Heaven knows how she knew where I was as I hadn't had the need to put the light on nor had I flushed the cistern or run any water yet. It was so off putting it made going to the toilet impossible.

Bit by bit, day by day, Ginny was invading our lives, invading our space and our privacy. Her continued verbalism was driving away friends and neighbours. Nobody wanted to visit us unless they were certain she was out. Everybody was becoming afraid. Talking amongst ourselves we had come to the conclusion that Ginny must have put some bugging device inside of our house. Either that or she had extra sensory radar ears. There could be no other explanation as to how she knew so much about current issues affecting our personal lives.

Once such instance had been when I was off sick with a chest infection from my job at the Intervention Board. She seemed to know an awful lot about it. The fact I'd been to the doctors, got a prescription and a medical note signing me off for another week. I hadn't had the chance to discuss my illness with anyone other than my parents, and even then not outside within Ginny's earshot.

I had to get away from it all. I had been forced to listen to her rabble on and off all morning, how being an evil person meant I didn't deserve health and happiness, how I must suffer and be punished for all the bad that I had in me. Ginny was clever with her words and definitely knew how to tune into my weakest parts at my weakest moments, and this last statement was far too close for comfort.

A year after leaving school I had gone through a rebellious patch, often landing myself in trouble with the police for petty crimes such as, drunk and disorderly, threatening behaviour, criminal damage and minor motoring offences, to name but a few. After one particularly frightening experience in court when I had come extremely close to a prison sentence, it suddenly dawned on me just how horrible I had become. I could see the ways my selfish behaviour was affecting those around me, the anxiety and pain I was causing my parents, the endless fights my sister was getting into defending me as her sister and the name calling she had to contend with. One time she was left crying on the doorstep after begging the police not to take me away again. She was just eleven years old, locked out of the house on an icy cold morning in just her flimsy little nightgown. That was just the worse thing I had ever experienced. I was supposed to be looking after her while Mum and Dad were at the shops. As the police car drove away with me locked in the back of it I felt my heart breaking to see my little sister so distressed. What sort of person had I become? As for the detective, well he should have known better. None of my family deserved to suffer in this way, yet amazingly they all stood by me.

    I felt guilty not only for my crimes but also for the way they were feeling, for being a failure and letting the whole family down. I felt like a bad person, rotten to the core and I knew I had to change my ways. Meeting up with my friends I knew would be fatal, resulting in further arrests. Therefore I cut myself off from everyone except my family and simply stopped going out. Subconsciously I stopped eating to rid myself of the excess energy building within. I went from extrovert to introvert, I became agoraphobic and anorexic.

    Over a two year period I tortured myself, each day convincing myself that I was an evil doer, not worthy of anyone's time, love or attention. I was a wicked spirit who deserved nothing more than pain and suffering. I detracted every ounce of goodness that was ever in me, filling my mind instead with only the bad things I had done. All I could see and all I could feel was a very deep self hate that I allowed to grip with such intensity, I had felt my life literally draining away. It had taken years of frustratingly hard work by me, my family, probation officer and doctor to get me back on track again and believing in myself once again. Until now I had gone from strength to strength.

Many years had passed since that awful episode in my life, but the feelings were beginning to resurface and be all too familiar. That morning for the first time, I had allowed Ginny to penetrate the protective layer I had created to isolate these feelings. I had allowed her words to enter my mind by taking on board her evil statements and churning them around inside of my head. The brain washing process she so obviously had in store for me was beginning to take effect. I once more believed that perhaps I was a bad and evil person after all.

Desperately needing to grip on reality and clear my head from such nonsense, I felt a walk in the fresh air would put me back in touch with civilisation. Absent minded, I strolled off in the direction of the shopping centre. I didn't give old Crackfart the satisfaction of knowing she had driven me out, although I could tell by the way she was excitedly hopping about, that she believed that she had. Instead I smiled calmly and looking directly into her eyes, I said, "It's a lovely day for a walk, don't you think Ginny?"

My deliberate actions had shocked her into a stunned silence as she obviously hadn't got the response she had hoped for. In all honesty I don't know how, through gritted teeth I had come across so convincingly, especially when what I really had the urge to do was to scream out, "You stupid bitch, can't you see you're the mad, evil insane cow, you're the one who needs taking away by the men in white coats. Can't you see what you are doing to people, what you're doing to me? People are turning against you; soon it will be you, all on your own, with nobody in the world to help you."

At the same time I would have been quite happy to have scratched out her eyes and voice box and stitched up her ever open mouth!

Having had my walk, collected my thoughts and stored them away again, I felt it safe to return home. I began to make my way out of the shopping area when this thick, blue, woollen winter coat came into view and began approaching me at some speed. *This can't be real*, I thought to myself, *I must be hallucinating*. Nobody in their right mind would be wearing such a heavy coat on such a warm and sunny day. It meant only one thing, Ginny was heading my way! To avoid confrontation I dashed towards the nearest shop front and pretended to be engrossed in their window display. I watched in the window as her reflection passed by, but I was too slow. Ginny, having spied her prey suddenly jumped onto the nearest bench and using her loudest, shrillest voice began shouting. "Excuse me, excuse me everyone, can I have your attention, your attention please, I have a very important announcement to make."

Everybody around seemed to stop, and was staring at this strange lady, when pointing me out, Ginny continued, "See that girl over there, Louise O' Down, the one with the bright purple top on. Well you all need to know that she has AIDS, yes that's right, you must keep away from her she is bad and evil and has AIDS. Yes Louise has AIDS."

The wobbly feeling I'd had soon went once the adrenalin kicked in and I ran faster than I'd ever run, helter-skelter through the record shop, into their store room and out through the back door. I had never been so embarrassed. All the way home I silently kept praying, please God don't let anyone who knows me have heard that, over and over, please Lord, please.

I think my main concern was that somebody from my work could have heard Ginny say that I had AIDS, and with my being off sick may have put two and two together and come up with three. It wouldn't have mattered that she was lying, once the story got out there would be no stopping the gossip mongers. Proverbs 18, verse 18 states *Gossip is so tasty, how we love to swallow it.* There's never been a truer word spoken.

Chapter Three

Ginny's behaviour gradually began to have an effect on everyone living within sight of her house. It didn't matter if you were old, young, middle aged and married, single or disabled, everyone had become a target and everyone would suffer. Ginny Crackfart, one woman in her early forties had waged her war in what was once a peaceful and happy neighbourhood.

Her actions were to affect people both physically and mentally. While some of us could still manage to have a good laugh over her bizarre antics, other could do nothing but let the anger and tears well up and overflow.

One of the first people Mrs Crackfart affected was my dear Mum. In my mind, Mum was a tough lady who could cope with just about anything life threw her way. Apart from going a tad green on a bus journey, she was never ill. A housewife for over thirty years, she was a big lady, large hearted with an equally large loving personality. She was always fair and independent in her thinking and always there for someone in need. Her door was always open, even when it was closed. Mum never appeared to be frightened about anything, and if she was she certainly didn't show it. For me, she was my comrade, a constant strength through the trials and tribulations of my complicated life.

When Ginny's actions began to include attacks of physical violence, it wasn't long before my once strong and fearless Mum became a quivering wreck. Each time Ginny would so much as rattle her back door handle, a trembling Mum would desperately head off for the bathroom. It soon became her second home as the abuse increased over the next four or so years. This aggression and at times extremely frightening behaviour of hers was no longer a laughing matter for anyone concerned. All concentration was devoted to avoiding the vast amounts of dangerously fast flying missiles that Ginny launched from her side of the fence.

It began with stones gathered from the borders of her garden. Smooth round pebbles that she had piled up by her back door. Two or three of these would be accurately aimed at people's backs, as they tried to weave a safe passage either in or out of our house. I felt like one of those vulnerable sitting ducks that bob along the wire on a shooting gallery at the funfair, and often wondered what prize Ginny thought she would win for getting three successful hits in a row.

For a couple of months this wicked woman seemed content with her pebble throwing verbal exercises and as nothing different occurred that had us unduly worried, we continued to ignore her attacks the best we could. Unfortunately the more immune we appeared the more ferocious her attacking became. The pebbles were replaced by rough jagged stones, which in turn were replaced by doughnut sized lumps of concrete, until finally she was slinging house bricks at us!

Agnes, one of our more elderly neighbours and Mum were the first to be picked on by Crackfart to play *Dodge the Doughnut*. Maybe because they both had bad legs, Ginny assumed they would be slower than the rest of us and easy targets to practice on. Agnes may have been in her seventies, but her love for gardening had kept her deceptively fit and agile, making Ginny's task that somewhat more difficult. She was a feisty old bird, was Agnes.

The day this game began, Agnes had popped into Mum's for a cup of coffee and a chat. The entire time they chatted, Ginny was verbally parading up and down her driveway, intensely upset by their obvious friendship. Despite the doors and windows being closed, every word that grating voice delivered could be heard inside of the house. When the time came for Agnes to leave, Mum decided to walk with her to the front gate, jokingly saying something about safety in numbers. This act of protection simply increased Ginny's excitement and the pair had hardly stepped outside when the witch began wildly pelting them with rocks. Intermittent wailing was accompanied by threats to have us all locked up. First Mum, then Agnes, then back to Mum, the rocks just kept coming.

Hearing all the commotion, both Dad and I ran outside to see what on earth was going on. By now Mum and Agnes were retreating back to the safety of the kitchen, although verbally they were giving as good as they got. Shouting back I suppose is a sort of defence mechanism, no matter how hard we all tried not to, at some point we all did. With Dad and I trying to calm the situation it must have sounded like world war three had erupted.

Both women had been hit by Ginny's missiles and although neither had been seriously hurt, they were both extremely shaken up. Now that the threats had actually become a physical reality, Dad was a little more optimistic about phoning the police. Surely they would put a stop to all this pointless aggravation. His optimism was short lived to say the least, unhelpful as on other occasions they said "There is nothing we can legally do, there are no independent witnesses and the attacks happened on privately owned land, sorry."

And so the excuses went on. Apparently if these attacks had happened out on the street and not over the garden fence, then the situation would be very different. To this day I cannot work that one out.

"We'll call by later to see if things have calmed down, you know sort of let our presence be felt." On that note they left. They didn't even go next door and speak to Ginny.

Anger welled up in our voices as we discussed the seemingly hopelessness of our plight. My parents went upstairs to get ready for a business meeting they were attending later that evening. Agnes had left with the police, and so I collapsed confused and defeated into an armchair. I needed to understand why this hermit had changed, why she didn't like any of us. What made her tick?

Deep inside me I was hurting. I wanted some retribution, and I wanted this old hag to pay for her actions. I didn't want to hear anymore of the vile she spat from her sneering mouth, abuse that clung to every fibre of my mind. There seemed to be no escape. Over and over I replayed the images and sounds of earlier, I just couldn't understand it. I couldn't bear to see my precious mum being set upon, to see her so shaken and frightened by this insane and cruel woman, but what could I do?

When the police had arrived, Ginny had cleverly disappeared

inside and although it was quiet now, instinct told me that it wasn't going to stay that way. As I imagined my counter attack I noticed dads boss Jim had arrived and was making the fatal mistake of parking right across Ginny's driveway. It would only have been for five minutes and it wasn't like Ginny had a car or needed access to that particular part of the road. All the same it was enough to set her off again, an excuse to once more make herself be not only seen but heard.

Making certain he was a visitor to our house she waited for the exact moment Jim set foot upon our driveway before launching her attack. Like a flash of lightening she miraculously appeared screaming and wailing. It was enough to scare anyone half to death. From her side of the fence she trailed Jim the fifteen or so yards right up to our front door, all the while swearing and cursing him, waving her arms to gesture threats of forthcoming violence. Ginny's voice would rise to a high pitched squeak as she almost choked on her words, then switch to a low deep growl as she once again tried to menace with meaning. *Where does she get off,* I thought to myself, *she has never even met this man before let alone spoken to him.*

I was not entirely sure, what if anything I should do. Would she turn on me if I tried to intervene? I wanted to rescue Jim but at the same time the coolness of his face told me he was not worried by her behaviour. I lingered at the window anticipating, wishing even for a confrontation to occur, one that I hoped Ginny would lose, then realised I ought to go and let Jim in.

I was very apologetic for Ginny's behaviour and my fumbled and embarrassed words must have made just about as much sense as Ginny's just had. Jim's straight face softened into a huge grin and he roared with laughter.

"Don't worry about it, I find the entertainment quite amusing, I've never had such a more welcoming greeting"

Dad however was not as amused, and as he so rightly pointed out they still had to get from the house back to Jim's car. Ginny had vanished just as quickly as she has appeared, but in the peace that followed an eerie atmosphere hung in the air.

After my parents had left I wandered around the house looking for something to do. The quietness was actually boring. The anger I had felt earlier had subsided and I felt a lot more relaxed. Lighting a ciggie I switched on the television and began flicking through the channels until I settled on a wildlife documentary that had me transported to some far off destination.

"C'mon out you mental cow. I know you're in there, you can't hide forever. I know you're alone, come on out and let me deal with you, let me sort out your mental illness"

Oh no! Not again, not now, I thought to myself. I rushed to the kitchen window and from behind the safety of the net curtain I could see Ginny. Her face contorted with rage, seemed to bore a whole right through my entire being.

"You need help, I know just how to string you up, I will get you sorted you see if I don't. It shouldn't be allowed mental cases like you being allowed to live in the community. You ARE bad and EVIL, come out now and suffer the consequences"

For twenty minutes I listened to this nonsense, anger once more welling up inside. My whole body was shaking and no matter how hard I tried I just couldn't shut her ranting from my ears, from penetrating my mind. My limbs filled with adrenalin and I had an overwhelming desire to do her some serious harm. I wanted to mash her brains in and shock the living daylights out of her. But within me I knew that this was not the answer, I knew it was what Ginny wanted me to do. It was so clear that she was inviting me for a fight, but I wasn't going to give her the satisfaction... well not in a physical form.

Or was I? My mind raced, so she thinks I'm afraid of her, how can I deal with this, how can I silence that filthy mouth? It seemed pointless phoning the police again. They hadn't appeared interested before; neither had they returned to make their presence felt as promised. To beat Ginny at her own game I would have to box clever, perhaps trick her into a false sense of security and power.

Then it came to me. Grabbing a bowl from the kitchen sink I quickly filled it with icy cold water carried it through to the hall, chuckling to myself. Carefully and ever so quietly I opened the front door just enough to let it rest on the latch, then sped back to the kitchen and in my loudest voice began to sing, "I don't care what the weatherman says if the weatherman says it's raining, you won't find me complaining."

Over and over I repeated this line. If old Crackfart thought I was mad, then I might as well act mad. I had nothing to lose.

Boldly I stepped out through the kitchen door and into the bright evening sun. It was a warm pleasant feeling and I felt supremely confident. Ginny couldn't help but express her delight and began clapping her hands together. She almost, but not quite, cracked a smile.

"Weakling reject mental waster, weakling reject your downfall is coming. Ha Ha! It's coming!"

Squaring up to her I continued to sing my song, all the while staring her straight in the face. Her words faltered as I tried to out sound her. She would jump back if I shouted loud, I'd jump back. If she came forward, I came forward. It was like a slow moving mirror image, but one that I was discreetly moving out towards the front garden.

"Weakling, reject, nobody loves you. They pretend but your parents didn't really want you. You are a mistake, you'll amount to nothing. You need your mummy but she doesn't need you."

Every other word began with an 'F' and finally I couldn't take it anymore. Our hip hopping verbal volleyball game had drawn us level with my front door. Suddenly I swung round, pushed open the front door and in one swift movement had the bowl of water in my hands.

"Yee haaa!" I yelled and charging down the driveway I delivered an accurate aim of lovely wet water right into the path of a now fleeing Ginny. She ran headlong into it and then came to abrupt stop as the shock sank in, the ice cold water making her splutter and gasp for breath. There was silence, an ear shattering silence where for a brief moment in time we just stood and stared at each other. Then, Ginny with a face like thunder turned on her heels and gabbled out a weak threat to call the police.

I didn't want to hang around to see what, if anything old Crackfart was going to do to me, but at the same time I didn't want to appear frightened by my own actions. Earlier in the day during one of her previous verbal attacks she had also leant over the fence and hacked away at Mum's ivy. She had discarded it on the roof of Dad's car. It still lay there, sadly scattered and dying where she had thrown it in a bid to make us react. Slowly and deliberately I gathered the cuttings and calmly walked back to the dustbin and laid them to rest. From her landing window Ginny watched me, but for once her mouth remained closed.

"Oh heck, what have I done?" I thought to myself. Behind closed doors I was now falling apart. I knew Mum would be upset and disappointed with me and Dad cross that I had retaliated. I couldn't undo what had happened, but what really ate away at my mind was the fact I had lowered myself to Ginny's standards. I had equalled her pettiness.

For a whole week there was this spooky sort of atmospheric calm. There was no more abuse, no shouting, no threats and no Ginny spying from her windows. In fact there appeared to be no Ginny at all. It was all so weird. We had all got so used to her behaviour that it had automatically become a part of our lives, it was expected. It felt like the house next door was empty, derelict with no signs of life. Perhaps my water throwing trick had actually done the job, perhaps it had bought Ginny to her senses and in her embarrassment she was keeping a low profile. Who knows, but the respite was a welcomed relief.

I had tried to put myself in Ginny's shoes, imagining how I would feel after acting out the way she had. Just thinking about it made my face flush and my insides cringe. I thanked God that I was not like her and asked should I ever become so, please send a giant whale to come and swallow me up.

Chapter Four

The next six months were to pass in a frenzy of activity. It was the first of many short, yet intense periods of persecutions that was to drive us all to distraction. Ginny's verbal battering became twenty four hours a day, every day for weeks on end. Physical violence occurred every time we left or entered the house. It was both frightening and emotionally draining. We began to feel like prisoners in our own home.

For us, myself mainly, it was also the beginning of a wild goose chase around the authorities, people and organisations who are supposed to have certain powers in dealing with such situations. It became a game of pass the buck, an absurd hopeless pursuit that continually ended in a confused state of total frustration.

To start this latest session of aggravation off, Ginny decided to dispose of her household waste via our garden. Hurtling over the fence at the speed of light would fly rotten fruit and vegetables, baked bean cans, half eaten shepherd's pie and the likes of other oven ready meals. On one occasion there was even a used sanitary towel. It was totally disgusting. Although we didn't always see Crackfart deposit these surprise parcels we still knew it was her. Often they would be launched from behind our backs as we entered the house. If you turned around quick enough you would just be in time to see the handle of her side door fall back into place. A favourite trick of hers was to jam pack a flimsy plastic bag, with a couple of small holes in it, so full of leftovers that it would literally explode on impact, splattering globules of rancid remains all over our back yard.

This was one of the things that really got Dad's goat. He liked to keep a tidy ship and whenever he could, would spend time sweeping clean the concrete areas of our back garden. Yet, no sooner had he put the broom away and stepped indoors the yard would once more look like a bomb had hit it. Ginny obviously used to lie in wait until he had finished and then make her move. Mum used to beg Dad not to go outside and antagonise the old witch by immediately clearing away the mess of which she had just deposited. This usually resulted in Dad surrendering to her pleas for calm and skulking off up to his office to await dusk, before being allowed out there to remove the rubbish.

If Mum and Dad were out when Ginny played the garbage game, I would clear up the mess the moment it landed and wash down the pathway before they returned home. I'd get a load of verbal flack and a pebble pelt for my troubles, but I rarely told my parents of the latest attack. It was worth it if it stopped Mum getting distressed and upset. She really was becoming quite wobbly about all the hassle.

We would continually talk about Ginny's rapidly increasing attacks and it had become the main topic of conversation in our house. We discussed the way in which Ginny dressed, the way she moved, the state of her property, her weird expressions and the anger in her face. Often she looked haggard and sick, unkempt and her body language was a tell tale sign that she was almost certainly suffering some form of mental instability. Nothing else mattered to us now except stopping this woman in her tracks. Some of the neighbours were also experiencing similar treatment to us, although not to the same intensity. We decided the time had come to seek professional help, both for ourselves and for Ginny. But where did we begin?

I trawled through the phone book looking for ideas as to who she may possibly have had contact with in the past. My first port of call was to the social services department. Nervously I rang the number and explained to the receptionist the problems we were having.

"There's nothing we can do, she kept interrupting, not our department."

Over and over she repeated herself, never really giving me the chance to complete a full sentence and although I tried to make myself heard it was a complete waste of time.

"Who's department is then" I asked

"Not ours, just keep phoning the police, it's up to them to deal with her, OK" then the phone went dead. What a completely rude and uncompassionate woman she was.

As their offices were based in the shopping precinct Dad decided he may get a more favourable reply if he were to visit in person. Off he went, confident, positive and determined. Some hours later he returned, having been kept waiting only to be told the exact same thing I had. He hadn't even been able to get passed the receptionist, let alone speak with a social worker.

Ginny's attacks continued. Pebbles, rocks, rubbish and foul mouthed verbal at an intense rate. She repeatedly informed us of her plan;

"I'll keep on and on at you all, until you are either locked up in Fairmile Mental Hospital, or arrested and sent to prison. I'll have you all, one by one. My attacks will continue. You can't beat me, I know how to play the system!"

Apparently she planned to wipe out the entire street. Each time she attempted her mission we called the police. Sometimes this would be three or four times a week, and each time we got the same response.

"It's just a domestic. We can't do anything. Call social services."

"We've called them and they say it's your job to deal with her as she is committing criminal offences."

"No, it's not us. You must call them. Try them again."

And so it went on with the conversations always ending the same way. To arrest somebody like Ginny, they needed evidence, to get that evidence they needed independent witnesses and a victims word stands for nothing as they are not independent to the situation. It would be the victim's word against the assailants and this being the case the Crown prosecution service would throw the case out before it even got to court. It was all about money and statistics. Unless a case had an eighty percent chance of winning, with clear evidence stacked against the offender, then it simply wasn't worth the paper it was written on. I knew the wheels of justice turned slowly, but now it appeared they had a puncture!

My confidence had taken one too many battering, I could no longer concentrate at work and I certainly couldn't sleep. My mind was a video recorder, forward, rewind, forward, pause, the day's events playing over and over in my mind.

I decided to once again have a go at getting some help for Ginny. This time I came across the district mental health unit and without hesitation dialled the number. I was prepared for battle to commence. To my surprise I was immediately put through to a care manager, who explained that Ginny was known to them. In fact she was known to all psychiatric departments within a forty mile radius of us. A statement this care manager later denied on the grounds of patient confidentiality, saying she was not known at all. During that initial phone call we talked for about twenty minutes and it was such a relief to unburden the whole saga to pair of very receptive ears. At one point the care manager even asked how I felt. He was on this first occasion very patient and understanding. The outcome of the call was that we had to start at the bottom of the ladder and he would get Ginny's GP to call in on her. He also gave me an out of hour's emergency number, should we feel the need for further advice or should Ginny go totally out of control.

It was about two weeks later that Mum saw the doctor from our surgery come sailing down the road on her bicycle, finally making that promised call to Ginny. Even though Ginny was in she wouldn't answer the door. Yet immediately the doctor left, Crackfart was out on her driveway telling us nobody could touch her and once again taunting that she knew how to play the system and how she would win. A second visit from the doctor some days later proved just as futile, only this time Ginny purposefully let herself be seen at the window. It was just another game to her.

Apparently if Ginny didn't want any contact with the authorities, mental health team, her doctor or the likes, then she had the right not to engage with them and could simply turn them away without reason. The situation was left with the police telling us that they would not intervene until somebody was hospitalized as a result of Ginny's behaviour, or Ginny herself contacted the doctors requesting support. It was both frustrating and frightening to realise we were totally alone in our struggle for safety, calm and peace.

It was two weeks after the doctor had visited that Ginny's first serious act of violence occurred. Coming home from work one evening on my motorbike, I noticed Crackfart out in her front garden. A prickly heat swept down my back and my stomach lurched. It was a hot day so I flipped the visor of my helmet up to let in some cool air. As I turned into the driveway and began to manoeuvre past Dad's car, Ginny suddenly came at me with a switched on Strimmer, jabbing and thrusting it right into my now unprotected face. Although it hadn't touched me it made me wobble on my bike. I could feel the vibration of its rotating wire cutter and the overpowering smell of freshly mown grass stung my nostrils. I struggled to stay in control as Ginny's hollow cackling laugh followed me around to the back yard, where once again she began to verbally crucify my sanity.

Frightened and shaken up somewhat, I flew indoors, wrenching off my helmet as I shot past Mum and grabbed the phone, still trembling I dialled 999 for the police. Surely now they would have to intervene. Shock sank in as I began to realise just how close I had come to being permanently disfigured.

In the few moments that followed this incident, Lynda was also making her way along the road. Being a good friend and neighbour she always waved as she went by. Even though we had nets which meant she couldn't see in, she knew we could see out. This wave was enough to distract Ginny from her attack on me and she set upon Lynda with a can of oil. At the exact moment Lyn passed her gates, Ginny began her squirting. The poor woman was not only covered in grease but was taking a right royal verbal battering at the same time.

Some minutes later the police arrived with blue lights flashing and sirens blasting. This was more like it I fumed. As usual Crackfart met them at the gate and in her most pathetic voice began to describe the events of earlier. She completely turned the story around. Whinging and wailing she was accusing me of attacking her, telling them how frightening it was and how she was now so frightened for her life. I listened from the kitchen window in utter disbelief. Surely they weren't going to fall for her lies again. Her strimmer was still out on the lawn, there was oil and grease all over the pavement and there was the fact that I had phoned for the police. Ginny had obviously done a good job as I was commanded to steer clear of her and let this domestic settle. I was seething.

    Later that same evening Dad bought a new car home and we were all excited. All my life I could only ever remember rusty old bangers, now here in front of us stood a gleaming, newish, shiny blue Fiat Croma. Some weeks earlier dads Renault had been written off by a driver who had jumped a red light. Thankfully neither of my parents was seriously hurt, but the shock of it had upset us all. It makes you realise just how precious and fragile life is. Dad was revving the engine of the Fiat, impatient for Mum to hop in and go for a spin with him. I wasn't good at being a passenger and managed to wangle my way out of the excursion. No sooner had the car set off when Ginny began taunting.

    "Your parents should have died in that crash, but God wants them to suffer, he wants to punish them by making them stay with you. Their brains should have been splattered in the crash, soon they will die and you will be left all alone and unprotected. DIE, DIE, DIE!"

    She continued to repeat herself until finally I snapped. To the left of me was our dustbin, its lid held down by a house brick. Without thinking what I was doing I picked it up and slung it at her with all my might. Ginny tried to dash through her garden arch but the brick caught her squarely on the heel. Realising I had just made a fatal mistake I fled the scene for fear of being arrested.

    Two police officers finally caught up with me at the youth club that I helped run on a Tuesday night. We were out on the back field playing a game of rounders, and their timing couldn't have been any worse. Two of the kids had just set fire to the playing field and being somewhat stressed that evening my rationale had evaporated. In a bid to put out the flames I was jumping about the dry grass like a kangaroo on hot coals, all the while screaming some not so pleasant threats at the boys responsible.

Waiting until the situation was under control, the officers then asked me to accompany them to the police car. I really thought I had been arrested. I believed my attack on Ginny had finally given her the upper hand and at that moment I hated this witch like woman with such intense passion, I knew, if she pushed me too far again then I wouldn't just stop at throwing a brick. I had never really hated a person in all my life. There were times of mutual dislike and moments of temporary coolness with people, but now I was filled with an angry hate. It felt like every fibre within my soul was drenched in a fire of hate, that was burning me alive, consuming my life in way nothing ever had, and I feared it would never go away.

As I sat in the police car explaining my version of events I realised I no longer felt remorseful. I was glad I had hurt Ginny, and although it was only a graze and bruising to her foot I knew I had made a statement. I believed Ginny knew it too. I knew these feelings were wrong and totally against all I believed, but I didn't care about the consequences. In the eyes of the law I had committed an offence, in the eyes of God I had reacted when I should have turned the other cheek. After all, her words were *'just words'*. I should not have allowed them to become a threat to me. I had finally crossed the line from the persecuted victim to equal.

Thankfully I was only given a warning on this occasion. The police were beginning to realise that perhaps this wasn't just a domestic dispute between neighbours, but a hate campaign by a very sick mentally ill woman.

Between July and December 1992, Ginny continued with the same pattern of events. Spasms of half hearted verbal were interspersed with physically aggression. One particular day and having badly missed her adult targets, Ginny resorted to throwing rocks at my friends' ten month old baby in his pushchair. Jo was one of the few people, who despite her fears, continued to visit us in our home. As she had made her way around to the back door Ginny had aimed, quite accurately at her sons' pushchair. One direct hit to the soft spot on his head didn't bear thinking about. We were horrified at the thought that her unrestrained nature had no qualms about targeting a defenceless baby, simply to continue her hate campaign against ourselves. Immediate action was needed to put a stop to all this disorder and as nobody in authority was willing to take a risk and help us, then we would have to go it alone.

Dad made contact with a solicitor, who in turn contacted the care manager of the mental health team, who then denied all knowledge of Ginny. We were advised that legally there was very little that could be done. This wasted exercise had cost Dad one hundred and ten pounds and we were no further forward. We could not afford to take out injunctions, nor could we afford any sort of civil action. It all seemed so hopeless again.

Somehow Ginny had homed in on our activity with the solicitor and seemed to find it both amusing and anger provoking. She switched tactics to that of tit for tat, and continually threatened to take us to court, shrieking with laughter at our own attempts to do the very same thing. During this period we also began to receive abusive telephone calls from Ginny. To begin with they were silent, but as time went on she began to shout and taunt us or perhaps play loud music down the line. It was yet another invasion of our privacy. It wasn't practical to change our phone number and go ex directory, as Nan, in her advancing years had started to become forgetful. She had dialled our number so many times that she no longer needed to think about it, it was so ingrained in her memory that her fingers just seemed to dial automatically. We were not willing to take the risk and expect her to learn something new, and putting that aside there was also all of Dad's customers to consider. It would cost a fortune, probably hundreds to inform them all.

Christmas Day proved to be a very testing time for us regarding the phone. Ginny made a total of fifteen calls from mid afternoon onwards. By early evening we had had enough and called the police. Our peaceful day had been shattered and the conversation had once again turned to the angry topic of Crackfart.

This was one of the few occasions that Ginny actually let somebody into her house. The police officer who attended spent quite some time in there with her. Whether he had a conversation, or was simply talked at, who knows, but when he came round to see us he looked very much the worse for wear. He told us he had considered getting her sectioned as she did indeed appear very unwell, but as it was Christmas day it would be very difficult, if not impossible to find a doctor, plus a psychiatric social worker or the likes to carry out this sort of order. So once again nothing more was done. He did advise us that if the calls continued he would get British Telecom to intercept the calls so we could then take Ginny to court. I assured him I would be down the police station for the relevant form the next time it happened. He warned that taking this route would not be a quick fix, but would indeed take many months to gather the evidence and get the case to court. It didn't matter, that bit of advice was the best Christmas present any of us could have asked for, and it gave us hope.

The officer had barely made it back to his car when the phone rang. We had half been expecting this of Crackfart as she could be so predictable at times. I answered it anyway just so I could log another call to help us in our quest. The second time it rang I picked up the telephone and let out a long, loud piercing scream. I scared the family witless so heaven knows what effect this had had on Ginny. Within minutes the policeman was back in our lounge telling us that Ginny had reported me, making allegations that I had assaulted her. It was kind of funny and in a way I suppose I had launched an assault on her, well her ears anyway. Obviously she still denied making the phone calls and therefore didn't make much sense in explaining just how I had done this. The police officer was at the end of his tether, not sure who or what to believe and left the matter at that.

Over the next few days the phone calls gradually decreased in intensity. Instead old Crackfart took to standing on her back door step taunting "You don't know what I've done! Ha Ha! You don't know, you don't know!"

This was weird behaviour as far as we were concerned as usually everything that came from her mouth was a direct attack about us personally. I did feel though she was trying to tell us something important about herself and somehow this filled me with dread.

After that we kept getting surprise visits from the police who claimed that Mum had phoned requiring their assistance. This was very strange and puzzled everyone including the police. The few times we had plucked up the courage to call them it was either Dad or I that did the ringing. Never Mum. Each time the police arrived and began to walk down our path, Ginny would fly out gabbling on that it was her that had called them. It all got very confusing. We never put two and two together for some time.

I can't recall exactly how we found out, but it appeared that Ginny had changed her name. I daren't reveal her real name for fear of recriminations. (Ginny Crackfart is simply the name adopted for her by my Nan because of the constant nonsense that spurted from her mouth). Ginny Crackfart was now to be known as 'Patricia O' Down'- my mother's name, my surname, the family name. She had said she would not ever answer to anything other than that. It was an horrific realisation. We were the only family in quite a large radius from where we lived that had that particular surname. People who didn't know the situation may now think we are all related.

By God I was mad. I went straight to the library upon finding out about this dreadful news and fished out the electoral register for our road. There it was plain as day, one Patricia O' Down at number twenty seven, and now another at twenty five. The electoral register comes out around October and we were now approaching spring, so Ginny must have organised this way back in the previous summer. I looked into this matter and there was absolutely nothing we could do to prevent her from using Mum's name. It is not illegal to take on another's name and Ginny now gloated with extreme joyfulness that this was soon to be rubber stamped at a solicitors.

Chapter Five

Most of 1993 continued with much of the same although at times to a more intense degree. Ginny's latest trick to entice me into battle would be to threaten to bash up my car. Another was to throw the rotten rubbish into our garden and then stand there with her fists raised, like a boxer, screaming;

"C'mon fight me, show me what you're made of, C'mon, bet I can beat you, c'mon and fight me, hit me, hit me, HIT ME."

Of course we never did, partly because it was wrong and probably more of a fact was that we were scared of her. There were times when I was so angry and could quite easily have jumped the fence and socked her one. It was just so hard to be restrained.

Ginny often used to target me when she knew I was alone in the house. I assumed she did this so as there were never any witnesses to her attacks. She was clever like that and probably knew it would be my word against hers and she'd get away with it. I was relaxing in the garden one sunny afternoon when she opened her bathroom window and began talking to me in a quiet, almost friendly way. There was no shouting or abuse, just simple everyday politeness. Although this stirred an uneasy feeling in me, I crept around the shed and peered up at her. Her face did appear much softer and that crazy wild look in her eyes was gone. She was less staring with her jaw relaxed. We stood and exchanged a few words before Ginny invited me to go over and sit on her wall to discuss 'the situation'. Initially this freaked me out, my insides churned and my heart pounded. I wasn't sure what to make of this offer but something was telling me it was an opportunity not to be missed. I considered the advantages and of course the dangers. She would be upstairs and I only a couple of feet away from the fence and so could easily hop back should she have another personality change. I told her I would be over in a few ticks. I must have been mad and although I was feeling brave I still had the common sense to phone Jo and tell her what I was about to do. She agreed to discreetly pop round in ten or so minutes, just to check I was ok.

So there we were Crackfart and I. She yakking from her window educating me about the facts of 'my' mental illness, and me perched on her 5 foot wall nodding like an obedient gnome. From the position I was in on my perch I could see past Ginny and into her bathroom. I noticed lots of tiles were missing from around the window and parts of the wallpaper were hanging in shreds. On the bare patches of wall were clusters of little notes written in different coloured pens. No doubt they were about me and my family. From what I could see the bathroom looked grubby and unkempt.

Apart from nodding my head and occasionally asking Ginny to expand on something, I sat there in silence and drank in all that she was saying. I managed to gain quite a lot of information about various organisations, therapies, and drugs relevant to 'my condition', of which I planned to investigate at a later date. It really helped me to understand a lot more about Ginny herself. I knew there was nothing wrong with me, but agreed with her anyway as I knew it was going to help me, to help her in the long run. It was funny. Her diagnosis of me actually appeared to be a mirror image, a reflection of the signs, behaviours and attitude she herself had been exhibiting this last year or so.

I was so absorbed in Ginny's lesson that I forgot about Jo coming round. Now, out of the corner of my eye I saw her come trotting up the driveway. I tried not to look at her as I desperately wanted her to stay where she was, to warn her away and keep out of sight. But it was too late, Ginny had already seen her. In that split second Crackfart reverted back to her wild and unrestrained nature. With eyes flashing she was like an erupting volcano as torrents of screaming vile abuse spewed from her ugly mouth. On and on it continued to pour out, getting angrier and more disgusting as each painful second ticked by. Then 'BANG', the window slammed shut and a deadly silence reigned. I was frozen in terror. Jo looked at me, I looked at her and neither of us spoke as we turned our gaze to Crackfart's kitchen door. The handle was beginning rattle and in that moment instinct told me to run. I fell from the wall, getting a little caught up as I scrambled the fence and fled with Jo to safety of mum's kitchen. My mind was in a whirr and I ran about like a headless chicken trying to find paper and pen. Schizoid personality, delusions, jealousy, schizophrenia and paranoia. I had to remember these words; they were a clue, the key maybe to all the persecutions we were suffering.

Although it was peaceful the following few days, I was unable to relax. I wondered if Ginny had realised I had been playing her, using our conversation to gain knowledge and understanding about her, rather than of myself. I had to keep reminding myself that it was indeed her and not me, that was so seriously unwell. My mind whirred day and night, imagining all the violent and wicked things she was going to do to me to get her revenge. I was frightened for my life; I had played a very dangerous game. Ginny had made many threats to my life in the past and now I feared that she would finally carry them out.

Something had to be done. I had to understand and be prepared. I grabbed my previously scribbled notes and headed off to the library. I had not told my parents of the incident on the wall and as I wasn't a library person, made out I was just nipping to the shops.

On arrival at the library I headed straight for the medical section and scanned the shelves for books on mental illness. Some of the titles I'd initially chosen appeared far too complex for the average person to understand, so I replaced these and settled myself down in a quiet corner of the library, with some that were a little easier to digest. I looked up the key words on my scrap of paper, in the books index and turned directly to that page.

Paranoia, whose main feature was that of delusions, seemed to fit the bill. The symptoms, feelings and activities of such a person can appear relatively normal, in that they are appropriate to their beliefs. In time anger, suspicion and social isolation may mark an increasing change towards difficult and eccentric behaviour. Umm...Ginny was certainly difficult and definitely eccentric. The sufferer rarely saw themselves as ill and usually only received treatment at the instigation of family or friends. But Ginny didn't have any friends, well not that we knew of, and nobody ever seemed to visit her.

My mind began to work overtime. One of us would have to be strong enough to befriend her, gain her trust and then get her the help she required to stop all the hurt and destruction she was causing. What an awful thing to do to somebody, an awful thing to have to do, and certainly not a good prospect for that one brave soul to undertake.

The book went on to say that suffers often had feelings of persecution which built up gradually by beliefs based on interpretation of chance remarks or events. These could include themes such as jealously, love and grandeur and was most likely to develop in people with paranoid personality disorder. These people were usually suspicious, over sensitive and appeared emotionally cold. It all sounded so Ginny, maybe she was simply jealous of our family and the lives we led. Perhaps she hadn't appreciated my wind up, that very first day that she had moved in, the one about the children's home. This could have bubbled and churned away in her mind all these years, finally resulting in her current behaviour. Who was to know?

Reading on I found the symptoms of Schizoid Personality Disorder were very much like that of paranoia. These suffers usually had the inability to relate to others and were often described as loners, having few friends, if any. They were markedly eccentric, lacked warmth and concern for others, were vague and apparently detached from day to day activities. All this didn't sound too bad. My interpretation of this was that it appeared the sufferer was in a world of their own. There was nothing to imply persecution of others and there was no mention of violence. What did worry me though was the fact that ten percent of sufferers went on to develop schizophrenia.

Schizophrenia is a general term for a group of psychotic illnesses and is the most common sort suffered. It is characterized by disturbances in thinking, emotional reaction and behaviour, and is often referred to as 'split personality', as sufferers' thoughts and feelings do not relate to each other in a logical fashion. This can be worsened by stress in the individuals' personal life and may begin insidiously with the sufferer becoming slowly more withdrawn and introverted, losing their drive for motivation. Change may not be noticed for some months or even years until the person suffers delusions, which dominate greatly. Thought disorders impair concentration and clear thinking, and self neglect can become a common occurrence. Ginny did occasionally appear unkempt, not exactly smelly and dirty but often wearing the same clothes for days on end. She was so very different now to her days of working in the city.

I drew to the conclusion that Ginny must have been listening to the voices of one of her 'personalities'. A personality that was commanding her - leading her to be abusive and to commit vicious attacks of violence, that made her lose control.

I was beginning to get confused. All these signs and symptoms seemed to inter-mingle with each other. In all of them I could see a little bit of Ginny, but at the same time I could a little bit in everybody else I knew, including myself. It also appeared that one illness could lead on to another, which for some resulted in schizophrenia. But where on this horrible ladder of chronic ill health was old Crackfart? Although I could now understand that she was indeed ill, it didn't make her behaviour any easier to accept. In fact it made me angry that she was allowed the freedom to cause physical and emotional pain to others, and all the while be protected by the legal system. My investigations led me to discover that there were actually panels of specialized solicitors, probation officers, court officials and the likes of others, in place to protect the sufferer from being mistreated by the justice system. Yet there was nothing to help, advise and protect the victims from such people who simply couldn't live in the community in a safe and acceptable manner. I supposed this is what Ginny was referring to when she said that she could play the system and win. It all seemed so unfair and so very wrong, and just confirmed my suspicions that we were indeed alone in our struggle to contain Mrs. Crackfart's behaviour.

A year had now passed since Ginny had undergone her personality change and the situation was far from resolved. Things were at an all time low and the revenge I'd feared following the conversation on the wall now came with force. Ginny could not have had more than two hours sleep a night for the entire month of April. Phone calls, rubbish, threats, silly rhyme singing, taunting, and of course the usual array of flying objects, and this was just the beginning. It was constant and I couldn't sleep. My bedroom window over looked Ginny's driveway and often in the small hours of the morning she'd parade up and down shouting horrible obscenities in the direction of my window. Sometimes she would talk with a deep growl, telling me how insane and bad I was. I would lie in bed with one ear buried in the pillow, pushing my hand against the other to try and block the irritating sound from my mind.

Quite openly Crackfart would gather ammunition, sometimes from our side of the fence. She would lean over into our garden, laughing as she did so and then proceed to deliver the stones back to their rightful place in our borders, via our heads. It got so bad that Mum, who normally didn't want to be directly involved, took to phoning the police herself. Recently she had called for their assistance twice within two hours, yet on both occasions received no proper response from them, despite being informed that they were on their way. In the meantime she was advised to stay indoors and either ignore Ginny, or go out and throw the rubbish and stones back. Both of these were seriously stupid suggestions that were more likely to inflame the situation, rather than calm it.

Out of the blue two officers came knocking at our door. Apparently Ginny had dialled 999 saying she was currently under attack from ourselves and was very scared. The fact we hadn't set foot outside the door didn't even come into the equation. It was amazing how quickly the police responded to her lies and false allegations, yet totally unbelievable that our genuine pleas were going unheard.

After much discussion and denials on our part the officers once again agreed that Ginny had a serious problem and promised that they would now get the inspector involved, with a view to setting up a case conference with social services. Hoping this would not only stop Ginny in her tracks, but get her the all important help she so obviously required.

All the time old Crackfart had been carrying on that day, I had recorded her on my cassette player. This I believe had helped the police reach the conclusion that we were in fact the victims and not the instigators of this so called domestic. Although this had been useful at the time of our discussion, one of the officers insisted, for my own good, that I destroy this valuable evidence as it was classed as entrapment and would prove useless in a court of law. Not wanting to jeopardize a positive outcome for ourselves I dutifully smashed the cassette and tore its ribbon to shreds before disposing of it in the dustbin. It was a month or so later that I was told, before the police could act they needed evidence and suggested I record Ginny's ranting. I was absolutely furious.

The weeks went by and there was no mention of a case conference and so being heartily sick of the situation I wrote to the department of Health in London, who replied:

'Firstly the patient must be suffering from a mental disorder as defined by the mental health act 1983, and that detention in hospital must be appropriate, requiring medical treatment and that admission to hospital is only made for the safety of the patient or for the protection of other persons'.

We knew this already and were actually hoping somebody somewhere would take that action in order to protect us and the neighbours. He also went on to say that he would contact the Director of Berkshire Social Services, asking them to personally look into the matter.

This director then passed the letters on to the local social services, who then passed them on to the manager at their sub office in Woodley, who replied to the MP stating that she had already advised us of our options regarding Mrs Crackfart and sais it was a police matter and that her department would not become involved unless Ginny requested them to do so.

So in the space of six weeks my letter had gone through four or five different departments and authorities and ended up back where I had started some six months ago, resulting in exactly the same answer. It appeared the ball was firmly in Crackfart's court and nobody was willing to stick their neck out and take some responsibility on our behalf. The plain fact of the day was that we were to be left unprotected in a situation that was frightening, dangerous and unbearable to live with.

This being the case then I decided I would have to fight fire with fire in order to prevent myself, my family, my friends and neighbours from coming to any harm, either physically or mentally by this cruel and insane woman.

Chapter Six

On my 28th birthday I woke to the sound of Ginny doing her wailing banshee act. She was prancing up and down the drive, banging her dustbin lid and throwing the odd insult across the fence.

It was Bank Holiday Monday, the sun was shining and I certainly wasn't going to hang around for a day of disruption. Mike, my boyfriend, suggested we spend the day at Windsor, and as he removed the roof of his little sports car I didn't hesitate. We sped along the country lanes, the wind blowing away the early morning cobwebs and ruffling my hair. I felt free. It was such a relief to be away from the house and for the next five hours I never once thought of Ginny. We had agreed earlier that this topic that dominated my life was a no go zone, it was not to be mentioned, and we whole heartedly stuck to it.

It was a brilliant day. We milled around the shops, mingling with the tourists, wandered around the castle and strolled along the river Thames. I sampled the delights of Häagan-Dazs ice cream topped with hot gooey fudge. Mike hired a little boat out and rowed me off along the Thames. At some point he must of taken a wrong turn, as we ended up down a very narrow side stream. Struggling to manoeuvre ourselves out we'd got somewhat tangled in the strands of the willow trees that draped themselves across the water. It was so funny and I laughed like I hadn't laughed in ages.

Driving home however, I began to get anxious. The nearer to Woodley we got, the more bad tempered I became. Mike pulled into the local Country Park and coaxed me into walking around the lake with him. He was trying so hard. He kept taking my hand and saying reassuring and lovely things to me, but I just felt more irritated by his affectionate distractions. I just wanted to go home now. My subconscious had prepared for battle and now I just wanted the forthcoming confrontation to be over with. Maybe that was a negative attitude on my part, but it was far easier to be living the hurt and destruction Ginny caused, rather than constantly be expecting the unexpected.

Karen was at the house when we arrived home and all appeared quiet and calm. Feeling brave the three of us took a cold drink and sat down the garden chattering. The sunshine was still warm and we couldn't have been laughing around for more than a few moments when there was this bang, bang crashing coming from Ginny's side of the fence. All heads automatically turned to the direction of the noise in question and there she was, two fists pounding the inside of her bedroom window. Suddenly Ginny flung the window wide open and began to scream and shout. On this occasion her anger was directed at Mike.

"You stupid boy! What you doing hanging around with that lunatic Louise? You could do much better, she'll drag you down, she is mental and evil, you should fear for your life".

This was the first time Mike had actually witnessed one of her outbursts, and while he looked a bit shocked, he continued to be laid back and encouraged us to ignore her and carry on as we were.

"Are you listening to me boy? Get away from them, that Louise has AIDS and Karen is a fat prostitute, you'll ruin your reputation. She is only using you because you've got a fancy car, leave now before it's too late".

Bang, she slammed the window and once again began banging from the inside. She was pounding so hard I was convinced her fists would shatter the pane and send millions of tiny shards of glass flying into the atmosphere.

"I'm watching you. I'm watching every move you make, everything you do. I'm going to the police to give them my evidence. Look you see, I'm gathering it right now!" And with that Ginny began to take photos of us all.

For the next hour or so there was Ginny click, click, clicking her camera, interspersing her evidence gathering with threats of physical aggression. It was beginning to make my blood boil but I was damned if I was retreating indoors. Mum kept coming to the kitchen door and in an unknown type of sign language repeatedly beckoned us to go in. But instead of obeying, Karen stood on a garden chair and began wiggling her hips about. It was hysterically funny and while I hummed the appropriate tune, she began to remove her outer garments of clothing and then continued in pretence to remove the rest. Mum was furious, Mike didn't know what to do and Ginny, well she was in raptures, clapping her hands, clicking her camera and whooping with glee. Karen had certainly put on a good show as a striptease act for the camera and it had dissolved my initial anger.

The next few weeks continued in the same manner, only now Ginny always had her camera to hand and took photos of us regardless of where we went or what we were doing. We had absolutely no privacy and I was forever angry and irritable. I so wanted to hit out but all I ever did was to occasionally give old Crackfart a bit of lip back. Then one evening while I was dreamily strolling along the road, I slipped on some gravel that had spread on to the pavement from a driveway. For some reason I recalled a conversation I'd had with Ginny back in the early days. I remembered her mentioning that she hated being alone in the house at night and hearing noises. My mischievous mind began to form a plan. I went back to the house where the gravel had tumbled on to the pavement and began filling my pockets, full to bursting, with the tiny little stones.

    That night I loaded some gravel into a catapult, switched off my bedroom light and lay in wait. About 11.30pm I could see Ginny in her kitchen. I reached out of the hopper window and aimed my weapon at her back door. "YES!" I exclaimed as the tiny stones flew from the sling and pinged off of the glass panel at the top of her door. Ping, "YES!" Ping ping. YES! Ping, ping .It felt so good.

    As I continued my attack I could see Ginny frantically running about her kitchen with her hands covering her ears. It was cruel I know, and very childish of me, but I gained so much satisfaction and more importantly, relief from my actions that I didn't care. I wanted her to feel how horribly exhausting and frightening mental torment could be, I wanted her to understand what she was doing to me and my family.

I had worked out that the weight of the stones was so little, that the force at which they hit her door made them bounce off of the glass in her door and straight back into our garden. I knew I could then whizz out and sweep them up without trespassing on Crackfart's land. I felt safe in this knowledge because should Ginny call the police there would be no evidence for them to find, thus making Ginny look all the more crazy than she already was. I was being a very horrible person and I did have the odd twinge of guilt, but not enough to stop me until all my ammunition was spent. I went off to work the next day having had a good night's sleep, with a smile on my face and a skip in my step.

For a couple of weeks after this retaliation by myself, Ginny gave us a brief interlude of respite from her persecutions. We could never fully relax and enjoy these moments of freedom though as her unpredictable nature meant we never knew when her next attack would come. Experience had taught us that when it did, it wasn't going to be a picnic in the park.

Ginny made her move at the end of May. It was an ordinary day and having had my tea I headed off for a shower. The mobile grinder had arrived in the street and quite a crowd had gathered around his van to have their knives and scissors sharpened. Job done Dad immediately returned to his shed, but Mum was lagging behind a bit after having a chat with the other neighbours out there. Ginny was obviously infuriated by this latest communal activity and came bursting out of her kitchen. Like a wound up Catherine Wheel she let rip with a frenzy of colourful, screaming abuse. I don't know whether it was the fact people were wandering around with dangerous implements in their hands, or whether it was simply the gathering of friendly chattering neighbours that had set her off, but something had got right under her skin.

Hearing the noise I came tearing down the stairs, half dressed I flew outside to check on Mum and Dad. I hadn't thought about what I was doing, instinct and the tone of Ginny's voice had told me this was serious. It was a fatal mistake. Crackfart had retreated behind her half open door and was hurling all manner of missiles in every direction possible. Clumps of congealed soggy food hit the window. It clung on looking for a grasp hold, slowly sliding and spreading itself, before finally falling to the ground in a dramatic death. Neither Mum nor Dad could get back into the house, and I had become an open target. Serrated tin lids flew through the air, their pointed sharpened tentacles slightly up turned, gleamed in the evening sun. It was terrifying. I had no choice but to make a run for it and managed to fling myself into our kitchen without being harmed. Grabbing the phone I dialled 999 and in short gasping breaths tried to explain what was happening. My whole body was violently shaking, pins and needles stung my face. I was hysterical and beginning to hyperventilate.

The police arrived in less than five minutes. The moment Ginny saw them her attack stopped, she ran towards them wailing and screaming for them to protect her as she was being assaulted by my family. She continued to act out a complete reversal of the true events and insisted I be arrested and locked up. I was by now emotionally drained and didn't have the will or inclination to argue the point. The main thing was that my parents had now managed to make it indoors, also without being seriously harmed.

The area beat officer – PC Granddad, as we'd named him – had now arrived on his trusty old steed. He wasn't the usual hands on type of copper like most, but preferred instead to pedal along on his bicycle waving at the residents and having endless cups of coffee with the oldies of the neighbourhood. His mission in life was signing them up for neighbourhood watch. With the situation now calmed the officers that had been first on the scene gave him a brief update and went on their way. PC Granddad then came into ours. He wasn't very forthcoming and said he had no intention of taking any further action. He shoved a piece of paper into dads hand with a mediation telephone number on it and suggested we give it a ring sometime. He then sailed away like a man without a care in the world.

That was it! I was not playing pass the buck any longer. I was supposed to be going up the sports and social club with Jo, but when I explained what had happened she agreed to accompany me to Reading Police Station. I was determined to make an official complaint about the way in which the police were handling the situation. For reasons unknown it appeared to be very one sided, in favour of Ginny.

I slammed the car into gear and put my foot on the accelerator. The tyres screeched as we shot away and the engine raced as I forced the gears through their combination at the speed of lightening, the mechanics protesting at my mishandling. Poor Jo clung on for dear life, not daring to complain and in no time we were standing at the front desk. I took a deep calming breath and in politest manner asked to see the highest ranked officer currently in the station. I was asked what my enquiry was regarding and after doing so was immediately told nobody was available, and to return on another day. No way was I going to be given the brush off and so pestered the desk officer until she made a call to the control centre verifying earlier events. She spoke for quite a while before again telling me to come back another day.

Feeling rather dejected Jo and I sat on the wall outside of the station wondering how we were going to get the attention we felt we deserved. It was while we were smoking our second ciggie that the perfect plan popped into my mind. Determined, I marched back up to the desk and informed the officer that if I didn't see at least an inspector in the next ten minutes then I would have no alternative but to chain myself to the front entrance doors, and by doing so would be preventing anybody else from entering the station. I also informed her that we would be calling the national newspapers to come and cover the story. This time we were asked to take a seat and no sooner had we sat down when an inspector came out and took us into an interview room.

At last, a pair of ears that was willing to listen without continually interrupting. This inspector was not best pleased by the treatment myself, my family and neighbours had received since Ginny had began her campaign and vowed to contact PC Granddad to get the ball rolling. He assured me that statements would be taken from anyone that had suffered in any way from Ginny's actions, and would call me in a few days to check how things were progressing. He thought maybe Ginny could be charged with an Edward the Eighth Bind Over, whatever that was, so things now looked hopeful. He also suggested that I keep a diary of events and take photos and recordings of Ginny in action. I couldn't believe what I was hearing. Only a short time ago I had been persuaded to destroy such evidence. He said I wouldn't be committing an offence and this information would enable the police to build a case against old Crackfart. I really believed everything he was saying and went away a far happier person than when I'd arrived there an hour or so before.

I hadn't told Mum what I had planned to do and thought perhaps I ought to give her ring when I reached the sports club. I need not have bothered. It seemed the inspector had already beaten me to it and spoken with Dad, and PC Granddad had arrived to carry out his orders. Apparently he was extremely angry with me for going behind his back and made it perfectly clear that he was not happy with the situation I had now put him in. I believe it was more likely that he was hacked off for being told what to do, and had no doubt been given a reprimand. Now he actually had to get off his lazy backside and do the job he was being paid to do.

Everyone did what they were supposed to be doing and a few weeks later Ginny was finally sectioned under the 1983 Mental Health Act. Initially this was for seventy two hours, but would be reviewed before a decision was made to release her back into the community. A meek and mild Ginny returned home four days later. She wouldn't look at anyone, and the verbal we had been expecting didn't come. She retreated like a tortoise into its shell and locked herself away indoors.

It was a blissful two months that followed. Then at the end of August, PC Granddad appeared informing us that no criminal charges were being made against Ginny and the case had been dropped. No explanation was given for this decision and as far as he was concerned the matter was now closed. I suppose I was a little bit angry and frustrated that I had only managed to complete half the job. Things had returned to normal so I agreed to let it drop.

This decision was indeed a tempting of fate. Ginny too must have been told she was off the hook and now obviously felt safe to once again unleash the monster lurking within her. In a smug and supremely self confident manner, she hung over the fence cackling and laughing, taunting us at our failure to bring her to hand. This was how it was to be, day after day. Very rarely did Ginny get dressed. Her days were spent parading the driveway in her dressing gown and slippers, throwing her missiles, screaming her threats and abuse. The mental torture continued and she reverted back to her face pulling days. The police would come and Ginny would lock herself indoors and then stare laughingly out at them from the window. The moment they left she was back out on the driveway continuing her ranting, but usually with more force. The police said no charges could be brought against her as she was unwilling to attend the police station for interviews, and anyway every time they attended Ginny had gone quiet on their arrival. She was quite clever like that. Invade, retreat, invade and retreat. It was all a game to her and anyway she could undermine our peace and happiness, she did.

One example of this was the little patch of garden than ran along the dividing fence out by our front door. It wasn't much, but it was all mine. I had been trying to grow vegetables in it and was often out there tending and watering my tiny plants. I was so proud when my baby carrots poked their leafy green tops up through the hard stony soil. There they stood, healthy and erect almost ready for picking. I always said 'good morning carrots' as I passed by them on my way to work.

One morning however, they weren't looking so perky. Their feathery green tops were now a murky grey colour and hung limply towards the earth. The soil around them was stained with a black greasy substance that had also splattered the paint work of our front door. I knew Ginny had done this as there were dribbles of the stuff running off of her concrete and on to my garden. I felt angry, but more so sad. Not only had she ruined my plants and contaminated the soil, she had once again entered my world and left her mark. Ginny had poisoned my carrots!

Chapter Seven

Home no longer felt like a place of refuge and harmony. A thick suffocating atmosphere surrounded the house and cracks began to show amidst the solidarity of our family unit. Endless discussions led to angry words as each of us aired our thoughts and opinions on how to handle the matter concerned. We had conflicting views as to what was best for us all. We knew we had to stick together and show a united front, but this in itself was becoming a battle.

The first words that passed our lips each morning concerned that of Ginny. Every meal time became an indigestible dispute and at bedtimes our minds were filled with imaginary conversations while re-running the day's events. We ate, slept, drank and dreamed Ginny Crackfart. It was becoming a twenty four hour occupation.

My brother would occasionally pop in for a visit and lord his great wisdom and authority over us, saying the answer is simple – IGNORE HER! How could he understand, he wasn't living the nightmare. Karen was a lot more sympathetic though and like myself wanted to march into battle and fight fire with fire. For Mum it was hard. She was around the house all day and if nobody else was at home she simply locked herself indoors. Some hot summer days I'd come home from work and find the washing drying in the back bedroom, instead of out on the line. Mum was just too frightened to risk antagonizing Ginny. I don't really know how Dad got through these intense and horrid years. He would appear angry at the time of an incident and a discussion would ensue, but then he seemed to simply shut down without showing any further feelings about it to any of us. I think perhaps by doing this he was trying not to let Ginny consume us.

It was September now and I'd had enough. Ginny had made allegations to the police that I had attacked her with a knife. I'd had to attend the police station where I was read my rights and officially interviewed on tape. I was not amused. I still get stressed and anxious if I have to go into a police station. The memories of the many nights I spent there, locked in a cell, during those six months of running riot as a seventeen year old, has had negatively lasting effect on me. Of course it was all suppositious nonsense as I had been at work at the time of the alleged offence. Work was where I always was these days. Being at work meant being away from Ginny and I took all the overtime I could get. I would tag a couple of extra hours on to my normal working day, then sign up for Saturdays and Sunday mornings. I always allowed myself Sunday afternoon off to go rambling in the countryside. The much needed fresh air cleared my head as I walked away any worries and frustrations that were lurking.

By the time I returned from the police station that evening, I was in a very agitated and bad tempered state. I could not get my head around the injustice being served up by both Ginny and the police. I had lost count of the many times I had been hauled over coals as a result of one of Ginny's fairy stories. It was unbelievable that despite knowing she was a total fruit loop they continued to take her seriously, while remaining deaf to our genuine pleas for help.

I had to get away. If things continued as they currently were I knew I wouldn't be responsible for my actions. Dad suggested Mum might like to come with me, and so within the hour we were booked into a hotel and on a flight to Jersey for the following Sunday.

The week passed slowly. I was both excited and nervous about our trip to the Channel Islands. I was nervous about flying but excited to be going somewhere new and away from old Crackfart. When Sunday did finally arrive it must have been the most atrocious day of the year. Swirling torrents of rain lashed down, being blown and tossed by gale force winds that made visibility almost impossible. The roads were jammed, motorways piled up with traffic at a standstill. Boats were docked, unable to sail and most long distance flights had had to be cancelled. We had caught the tail end of hurricane Hugo, which had blown in from America.

A half an hour before we were due to leave I was checking teletext for the latest weather updates when there was a knock on the door. A reporter from the local paper stood there saying he has been told we had a story for him. Only because the weather was awful did I let him in. Ginny and her sixth sense had homed in on our activities and as usual had pulled out all the stops to put a dampener on our excitement. She had told him we were mentally ill neighbours from hell and as normal had reversed the truth to fit her fantasy. Despite his persistence not one of us gave him an ounce of information, neither agreeing nor disagreeing with his statements. It was simply a matter of reiterating to him, that he contacted the inspector at the local police station for further advice. It was not until we were loading the car and ready to set off that he finally gave up and went next door to Ginny.

On this occasion Ginny hadn't succeeded in ruining our plans. Our flight went ahead and Mum and I had brilliant five days away. It was a quiet time and especially good not to have Ginny chewing up our brains and spitting them out. On our return the remainder of the year passed with the normal ups and downs of life with Ginny.

Chapter Eight

1994 dawned with Ginny expanding her aggravation and tirade of assaults on anyone who dared to breathe within a hundred yards of her home. Her denunciations became a daily event again, both to us and by phone to the police. If they took little notice of her she would simply turn up in person at the station and cause a scene.

She began this phase of her crazy game by assaulting anyone she could get her hands on, and it didn't seem to matter where this happened. Coral and Agnes had been ambling around Waitrose Supermarket on New Year's Eve when Ginny came flying down one of the aisles, and like a bat out of hell and began ramming Coral in the stomach with her trolley. Having just had an operation on her abdomen, this physical attack had quite obviously hurt. Coral is normally the type of person that that does not take any crap, of any kind from anyone, but on this occasion she was so shocked and upset she simply went home and forgot about the shopping. Later though as events began to sink in she became angry and reported the incident to the police. She was told that because she hadn't reported the assault to the store manager at the time of the incident then nothing could be done. She did try and push the matter in the hope of an arrest but the police wouldn't budge an inch. They did say they would take a statement to add to 'the file' for future reference. What a load of rubbish, it was just another lame excuse for them to avoid dealing with the problem. Needless to say the statement was never taken and the incident was never mentioned again.

Having got away with it once again, Ginny's confidence grew and a few days later she punched another neighbour in the back who just happened to pass by her on her bike. The punch was so hard it almost sent

Gail tumbling to the ground. She was too frightened to report this to the police for fear of further attacks. So it was another victory to old Crackfart. But her luck was about to change.

One cold February morning Jo was returning from the shops with her youngest son, 3 month old Leo, and as she wandered along she suddenly spotted Ginny walking towards her with a huge big grin on her face. Gripping the handles of the pushchair she decided to keep walking while looking at the ground so as to avoid all eye contact, and ignore the approaching Crackfart. As the two women drew level Ginny struck Jo across the chest and then laughed in her face when Jo spun round to look at her.

I was furious when I found out and made it my business to ensure Crackfart was punished for this. I pestered and pleaded and begged the police to take action, making a right nuisance of myself in the process. How dare my friend be assaulted simply because she continued to associate herself with me. She had remained a good, supportive and loyal friend throughout these years of trouble, and now I felt so guilty that she should be attacked and punished for being so.

Four days later and after a lot perseverance by Jo, her partner and myself Ginny was eventually taken to the police station and interviewed. This time she wasn't given the option of whether she attended or not, she was just taken. As she flatly refused to utter a word, even in her defence, she was arrested and charged with assault, then bailed to await a court hearing.

A month later Ginny stood in the dock and pleaded not guilty to assault, meaning Jo had to go into the witness box. There weren't any other witnesses, so it was her word against Ginny's. Jo was an absolute nervous wreck and I suggested to her that it would probably work in her favour if she let a few tears drop.

My suggestion worked wonders and despite Ginny making out she hadn't a clue as to why she was in court, and at one point pulling out some underwear as evidence that she had been shopping on the day in question, she was found guilty. She was given a one year conditional discharge, fined eighty pounds and ordered to pay Jo twenty pounds in compensation for the distress she had caused.

It was brilliant. The conditional discharge meant that if Ginny committed any further offences within the next twelve months, they would be down on her like a ton of bricks. Her performance that day had been one of excellence. How I had refrained from laughing out loud when she'd pulled out the underwear, I'll never know. Ginny had kept repeating that she did not understand the proceedings. She denied all knowledge of Jo and said she was only aware of me through name only. Ginny claimed she had only learned of the troubles between herself and the neighbours through files given to her by Social Services.

The story had been so bizarre that it was reported in two local papers. One headline read *Recluse in court after slap attack*. It went on to say that Ginny had adopted our name some months earlier as she had thought it was prettier.

She was obviously very proud of her appearance in court as these articles were blown up on a copier, which she then stuck up in her front window for all to see and read. She thought the whole episode was extremely funny and continually taunted us that it was just the beginning and that nothing else would happen to her.

Nothing much did happen for the next couple of months. Ginny had begun to leave the house at around six thirty in the morning and wasn't usually returning home until after seven in the evening. This at least gave mum a bit of freedom and peace, and we all began to relax a little during this time. Curiosity and fear was eating away at me though. I needed to know exactly where she was going and what, if anything, she was doing that would affect us at a later date. My brother discreetly followed her one morning and discovered she was catching the London link coach. He trailed the coach right into the city centre but lost Ginny when she disappeared into a building while he was trying to park the car.

These London trips went on for at least six months but it didn't make a lot of difference to our evenings and weekends though. It appeared Ginny never slept. She often kept me awake at night with her purposeful banging and shouting out on the driveway. I was exhausted before I even got to work. In the beginning my workmates used to pounce on me the minute I arrived in the office, wanting the next instalment of the Crackfart saga. It was a great release for me, having a good moan about the mistreatment I was enduring, but as time went on people lost interest. I think it had become boring and at times so farfetched, I'm sure they thought I was making half of it up. Some said they wouldn't put up with it, others suggested I smack her in the mouth or move away from home. They said I'd do this or that and it was easy for them to talk tough because they weren't living the nightmare. They had to live it to understand why I argued their suggestions were not possible. There were many a heated discussion in the smoking room or down the pub with my mates.

There was a very fine line of the law that nobody except myself and my family appeared to appreciate. Basically, Ginny was not classed as sane and apparently didn't know what she was doing, and therefore could not be prosecuted for her actions....Yeah and I've got two left feet...we, on the other hand were looked upon as 'balanced' and were responsible for our actions and temporary insanity was not an option for us, no matter what stress and abuse Ginny put us through. That meant we could be charged with any retaliation that breached a criminal offence...even from our side of the garden. Yet, despite her insanity Ginny was not insane enough to be detained in a mental hospital. This law was insanity itself and the more I tried to understand the reasoning for this, the angrier I became. It really was total madness.

I did receive some emotional support from my church fellowship, but even they appeared to lose interest, and didn't really pay attention when I tried to talk out my fears and worries. I always seemed to get the same one line response, 'Give it over to God'...That was it, conversation closed! I had never felt so frustrated, angry, frightened and alone as I did at that moment in time.

Ginny's persistent persecution was not only messing with my mind, it was making me physically ill as well. I was beginning to take a lot of time off work. I took the opportunity to catch up on sleep during the day while Ginny was out of the picture. Over the years there were many night when I parked my car up at Woodley roundabout in a bid to grab a few hours sleep away from the noise. The police got used to seeing me there and often popped by to check I was alright. They too were now getting hundreds of phone calls from Ginny every night, I couldn't understand how they could let her get away with it...she should have been charged with wasting police time or something. The officers took it in turns to man the phones as they couldn't handle a whole night of her ranting. Each time they hung up on her she would immediately redial them. Some nights if it was quiet on the beat, the officers and I would sit and chat and smoke the night away. It became quite a sociable event.

There were a couple of occasions in the early hours of the morning when I had doused old Crackfart with a bucket or two of water. I didn't care if the police attended, I would have just denied it saying she had done it to herself, or perhaps tell them I had thought it was a cat howling in the night. So what if I got arrested, I had to do something to release the pressure of frustration within me.

One evening Karen and I were in the kitchen making some tea when Ginny came scooting out of her back door and grabbed her dustbin. She emptied its contents all over her own driveway and then strategically planted some bricks around the mess.

Karen and I jokingly estimated how long it would be before the police arrived. It was barely five minutes. Ginny met them on the drive and instantly went into a garbled frenzy accusing the pair of us of doing it, while we had been attacking her.

Without thinking I marched outside to defend myself and was closely followed by the rest of the family. I think they all sensed this was going to turn nasty. Crackfart was screaming at me to go over and pick up the rubbish . I was willing to oblige and made moves to hop over the fence. Dad was verbally trying to calm things down, while the policewoman was trying to prevent a full scale punch up, as the tension grew. Then very calmly and in front of everyone, Ginny leant over the fence, picked up a brick from our yard and hurled it with all her might at our front door. Her aim was not that accurate and it only chipped the bottom of the door frame.

"Yes, now you have to arrest her, she has done criminal damage in front of you, you wanted witnesses, now YOU ARE the witnesses, arrest her, arrest her and take her away" I screamed.

Crackfart headed straight for her back door in an attempt to lock herself away inside, but the policewoman was too quick for her. She jumped over the fence and grabbed the keys from Ginny's hand then swiftly locked the door from the outside. Ginny went into hysterical overdrive as she had nowhere to run and hide and I was still hop hopping about like a mad march hare shouting "Arrest her, arrest her, c'mon take her away, enough is enough"

There were only seven people involved but it seemed like there were dozens tearing around. It must have looked like a clip from a carry on film.

The police calmed things down a little, but told us they were not going to arrest Ginny. Upon hearing this I flew into a riotous rage and lunged towards the fence with every ounce of strength that was within me. Both policewomen were trying to restrain me and were dragging me out towards the front garden. I fought them all the way, shouting and swearing I was totally out of control. Never would have spoken like that in front of dad, never in a million years. Dad was begging and pleading for them to let me go. After being locked up in the police cells as a teenager, I think he knew how I felt about being trapped, restrained or confined, and he could see their actions were making me worse. I was fighting them now, fighting to break free.

Eventually they did release their grip on me and I dived straight into my car revving the engine with anger and force. One of the officers stood behind vehicle in a bid to prevent me from driving away. Again Dad pleaded with them to let me go, saying I would go off and calm myself down. Finally she trusted his judgement and I sped away, shaking and crying. The unexpected temper that had risen so quickly within me had both shocked and scared me. Driving along I could still see Ginny in my head, clapping, jeering and laughing at my distress. I was still angry, but more so with myself now for giving that old bag the satisfaction of seeing my weakness, seeing my distress.

It was about two hours later before I had the courage to return home. I had walked twice around Southlake and smoked myself half to death in this time. I was relieved to see all was quiet and cook-a-hoop to discover that the police had returned and arrested Ginny after all. She was detained at the police station and appeared in court the very next morning. As she would not co-operate the case was adjourned until the coming Friday.

That Friday I sneaked out of work and went to the court to find out what was happening with Ginny. My office block was only a hundred yards or so away from the courthouse and I hoped I wouldn't be missed. Ginny spied me the moment I entered the building and got in a flap stating that she now feared for her life because I was there. She kept hysterically repeating that she needed protection. When her case was called I sat quietly at the back bemused by the proceedings. Ginny continually interrupted, causing total confusion for all concerned. She was warned that her behaviour would not be tolerated. Again she made out she did not understand what was happening and that she was 'on her own' asking if somebody could please explain things. I knew she knew what was happening and so did she. It was just another of her tactics to play the victim and prove temporary insanity in a bid to get off the charges. Throughout the thirty minutes Ginny kept saying I was going to kill her when she left the court and I was eventually asked to leave the building. It was a flipping cheek that yet again old Crackfart had got her own way by manipulating everyone involved with her case. I rang the court on my return to work and discovered that the criminal damage charge had been dropped and a bind over had been given. Meaning she would have to keep the peace for one year or pay a hundred pound fine.

So much for the conditional discharge she had received earlier in the year. The magistrates hadn't even taken that into consideration. They had apparently done whatever they could to get her out of the court so they could continue with the other cases listed for that morning. For weeks after this court appear Crackfart made numerous allegations against me, all of which I had to attend the police station for interview. Luckily, as the truth will have it, no charges were brought against me. It was worrying and stressful at the time though and I was feeling very unwell and exhausted, I also felt like I was going round the twist.

After a particular bad week I couldn't take any more of it. I had been off sick from work for some months now and in all this time there hadn't been a moment let up from Ginny. I desperately needed it all to stop. I drove myself to a railway line on a quiet winding road on the edge of Woodley. I clambered up on to the iron barriers of the bridge and drank a quarter bottle of vodka. I didn't normally drink and it seemed to go straight to my head. I wasn't totally drunk or even that sleepy, just a bit fuzzy headed and away with the fairies.

    I can still see that night plain as day. It was midnight, the air was warm and the only sound was that of a bird singing in the nearby trees. I remember thinking how odd that was – I had never heard a bird sing at night. As I listened I saw this huge round light appear someway off along the track. It was hypnotic, the light, the bird, the rhythmical rolling of the approaching train wheels, it was saying *'you can do it, you can jump. You can do it you can jump'* – faster and faster it came and the light seemed to grow in size and intensity. It made my wildly beating heart thump harder within my chest, and my head throbbed until I was at screaming point. When I couldn't bear it a second longer I launched myself into the air. A buzz of adrenaline seared through my pulsating body and the moments that followed were that of total confusion. What was happening? I felt an intense pressure upon my arms and my left leg. A vice like grip had clamped itself to my limbs and I was being somersaulted backwards and upwards. I should have been plunging down. I felt my floppy right leg smash against the iron work of the bridge before suddenly being hurled and bundled to the cold hard ground. This wasn't right. My voice seemed distant as I kicked and screamed and struggled to break free, I fought like I never had before. Then suddenly every ounce of energy drained from my body and I collapsed limply back, defeated.

    In my earlier daze I hadn't realised that somebody had cycled across the bridge and seen me sitting there. They hadn't stopped to talk to me but had hurried home and called the police instead, whose arrival I had also been unaware of. Two policemen had quietly crept up behind me and it was while a decision was being made as to do, had I launched myself from the bridge. Being only a few feet behind me they had managed to grab me mid flight and sling me to the ground for safety.

    I began to sob uncontrollably. As I looked around me I could see both ends of the bridge had been blocked by police cars and I realised I was now trapped. As I sat there a friendly voice began to talk to me, she called me by my name. I was in such a state of unreality and didn't really know what I was saying or doing. As my eyes began to focus through the tears I realised it was one of the policewomen that had restrained me earlier that month back at home. Somehow she managed to coax me into the police car and I was taken off to Reading police station. Once there I was seen by a doctor who amazingly said my actions had been a moment of desperation and that moment had now passed. He deemed me fit to go home. He didn't think I was any longer a danger to myself. Thank God! As I look back on that moment in time, I realise just how close I had come to handing Ginny the ultimate victory she craved, my death, or at the very least, sectioned under the mental health act.

    I was taken home by the policewomen, who then helped me explain the events of the evening to my parents. Both knew I had been struggling with old Crackfart's persecutions, but they hadn't realised just how bad she was affecting me. Mum was in tears at this point and kept saying;

    "Oh my little banana, my little banana, thank heavens you're alright. Sit down while I go and put the kettle on, Oh my little banana"

    I know my near departure from the world had come as a shock to her, but I cringed then, and still do now when I remember those words. As a grown up twenty-something it is far from cool being called a little banana, especially in front of the police.

    One of the officers had taken Dad back to the bridge so he could pick up my car. The other had stayed and discussed the general situation with us. We flung some ideas around as to what we or others could possibly do to try and tame the wild Ginny. Funnily, I felt somewhat relieved to be back home again. Yes the moment of desperation had indeed passed, and as I lay tucked up in the safety of my bed that night, I vowed never again to allow Ginny Crackfart to get me into such a state. My life was precious, I WAS a good person and I deserved to be happy.

Over the next couple of years though, there were terrible times when I forgot that promise to myself, when I wished for nothing more than to be dead. On a couple of occasions I actually took steps to take my own life again, simply because I couldn't cope with the confusion and madness caused by one very sick and at times evil woman.

Chapter Nine

Over the next two years Crackfart's behaviour was to reach its peak. She excelled with her tales of woe, and her fairy stories of my so called aggression and attitude towards her became more exaggerated and violent.

The police came and went on many occasions, rarely taking any action on our behalf, but at the same time doing their best to ignore Ginny's allegations of threats to her life. Of course they had to attend just in case she really was under attack, but once they realised she was in no danger they wasted little time in beating a hasty retreat. I believe they only turned up because they felt obligated to do so. Given the choice their sense of duty would have gone right out of the window. I really felt they were still not taking the situation seriously and it certainly came across to us all at they were fed up and totally disinterested with the ongoing saga. It was alright for them; they could go home at the end of a shift and try to switch off from Ginny. We on the other hand were still living the nightmare twenty four hours a day. Knowing the police really weren't interested in the troubles between us was really worrying me. Karen had set a date for her wedding to David and I feared that Ginny would go all out to ruin their big day. With no support from the police in place to prevent this I had visions of it ending in total disaster.

Since Ginny's name change it had become difficult for the police to establish who had rang and requested their assistance. Upon their arrival the police simply took potluck as to which household to attend first, and this in itself usually provoked a confrontational anger for all involved. If Ginny didn't get the appropriate response she expected, she took down the identity numbers of the officers concerned and made a formal complaint to the inspector about them. There came a point when there were so many internal investigations going on, all at the instigation of old Crackfart, that there were no Woodley officers allowed to attend our addresses. This meant that the Reading crew had to respond and being that much further away resulted in a longer response time. Not only was this frightening when we were threaten or under attack from Ginny, it was frustrating having to explain the situation over and over again, as it was always a different pair of officers that showed up.

During this two year period the abusive and silent phone calls from Ginny became more intense. One am, three am, twelve noon, it didn't matter to her. Clusters of calls, sometimes as many as fifteen in a row came day after day, until eventually we couldn't stand it any longer.

On the advice of the police I filled out a nuisance call complaint form and a couple of days later a trace was put on our phone line. It was so easy to use. Each time Ginny made a call we immediately pressed a certain digit on the phone pad and the trace was started. It meant we couldn't put the receiver down straight away as the trace needed twenty seconds or so to pick up the caller's number, so we had to listen to what ever rabble she decided to send down the line. Once the callers telephone number had been traced its details were recorded at the BT exchange. After a set period of time this information was then passed back to the police along with the person's identity who was registered to the traced number. As expected this turned out to be Ginny Crackfart. She was arrested, charged, and then released on bail until the case finally got to court. This was some six months later. During these six months the trace had been left activated and we received further calls that were also presented as evidence.

Two telephonists from the Northampton nuisance call bureau, Mum, and myself had been summonsed as witnesses. Along with Karen and Dad the six of us were squashed into this stuffy little room set aside to keep the witnesses and the offender separated until the case was called, Karen, not being directly involved was to be our mole. We wanted to know what went on from beginning to end, and as soon as the case started she took up position in the back of the courtroom.

Forty five minutes passed before my name was called over the tannoy requesting I go to court one. An usher met me at the door and led through into the witness box. It was absolutely silent in there and I felt all eyes were boring into me. My legs felt like jelly and my tummy churned as I took the oath. I hated being in situations where I felt trapped, and right then, standing in that box a couple of feet above everyone else, directly facing Ginny, I felt a rising panic that made me want to throw up.

I'd had a problem with my pituitary gland that year and as part of some tests I had been taken off of all medication for a three month period. The court case fell six weeks into those three months and I was feeling just awful. I couldn't concentrate. I had to make a quick decision. Did I throw up and risk making a fool of myself in front of everyone or did I break my pill free zone. One look at Ginny and her beige shopping trolley full of so called evidence against me, had me reaching for a couple of anti-emetics, which I discreetly placed in my mouth and swallowed. The moment I did this I felt regret. I was so angry with myself for being such a wimp, but the even deeper angry hate I felt for old Crackfart at that moment for putting me in this dilemma, is indescribable. It was a another victory to her, another way in which she had wangled her way into my life and disrupted it, on this occasion probably unknowingly.

My evidence was to take over an hour to give. Ginny had decided against legal representation, preferring instead to defend herself. It was a bizarre situation. For the most part of that hour she was allowed to question me in such a manner it felt like I was the one on trial. She kept delving into her shopping trolley of evidence, routing around before producing scraps of paper on which she had prepared her notes, and would then continue. My emotions were all over the place. At times I got internally angry and frustrated at what appeared to me, to be unjust behaviour. She would say something totally irrelevant and I would feel the tears well up in my eyes, making me want to run from the courtroom. A split second later she would say or do something else and I'd be doing my best to contain the bubbles of laughter brewing inside of me. It was so exhausting. I didn't dare look at my sister. We could never sit together in any serious or quiet situation without erupting into fits of the giggles. Even in church we had to sit staggered and separated, as eye contact of any kind would set us off. Now being so nervous and emotional I knew that if I did glance her way, the pair of us would end up in a hysterical heap. Even the prosecutor and the magistrates were struggling to hold themselves together at times, as most of the questioning I received was totally off the planet and irrelevant to the nuisance calls case.

"Are you the owner of a white ford fiesta, registration number F655 SJB?"

"Yes"

"Your car was missing for two weeks. Where were you between the 23rd of May and the 7th of June?"

I looked at the magistrate. Surely I didn't have to answer these nosy and demanding questions. It was so obvious she was digging for information about me and I didn't want to hand her all my secrets on a plate.

"You don't have to answer that Miss O' Down.

"Mrs Crackfart, will you please stick to the relevant facts of the case?"

Without even glancing at the magistrate she continued. "Do you live with your parents and suffer serious delusional mental health?"

"No, I am NOT mentally ill, that is you."

"You do don't you, I know for a fact that you ARE mental."

She was asking and answering these statements herself without even pausing for breath. She never gave me a chance to respond half of the time. My mouth was opening and closing but no sound was coming out, I must have looked like a muted Pac-man.

"This mental illness you suffer Louise, it makes you act aggressively towards me, doesn't it? You are out to get me, you need help and you attack me don't you?"

And so it continued. The head magistrate kept reprimanding Ginny, but she would ignore him and raise her voice to blot his out. What with that and the prosecutor bobbing up and down saying 'I object' every few seconds, the whole ordeal was doing my head in.

"You say this supposed neighbour 'Mrs O' Down' is making nuisance calls to your house in the middle of the night. How can you know this? You can't know, you are on medication from the mental hospital so you'd be asleep, I am right aren't I?"

"No, you are wrong. I have to go out in my car to get some peace and quiet and sleep. I didn't take sleeping pills then, neither do I now. So I am fully aware as to who is making the calls Mrs Crackfart. It is YOU" I replied pointing to her as I said it.

I deliberately called her by her real name as I did not want people thinking we were in any way related.

"On some occasions you scream down the phone at me, don't you?"

This was brilliant. She was dropping herself deeper into the mess she was in fact trying to wiggle her way out of, and my confidence was growing.

"You were ordered to see a psychiatrist because of all these phone calls. It made you more insane, didn't it?"

"I object"

"You don't have to answer that Miss O' Down"

"No, no it's fine. I really would like to on this occasion. Yes I went to see a psychiatrist but not for myself. You see I was given the opportunity to discuss the behaviour of my neighbour, that's you Ginny, and I was advised on how best I could cope and deal with the mental health problems you are currently exhibiting"

Upon hearing this Ginny flew into a terrible rage and totally flipped her lid. She came haring out of the dock and in her haste the wheels of her shopping trolley got caught up in the dock door. She huffed and puffed and tugged at it while still trying to convince everybody that I was the mental one.

"Look, look, here is the proof Louise is going to kill me. She needs help, she needs locking up. Section her, section her, she's going to kill me, she is mental. And get that girl out of the courtroom"

Ginny pointed towards my sister, then continued,

"She's a part of the conspiracy too, I want her out, now! I can't carry on. Protect me! Protect me!"

The magistrate had finally had enough of her play acting,

"If you don't get back in the dock and calm yourself down, I will hold you in contempt of court and you will be taken to the cells downstairs. DO YOU UNDERSTAND?

Throughout the rest of the proceedings Ginny's attitude and

behaviour constantly changed. While defending she acted cool, calm, sane and rational. Yet the minute she didn't like something she didn't want to hear, all hell broke loose and she played the 'I don't understand' card again. Eventually I recounted events surrounding the nuisance phone calls we had received and was discharged from the witness box. I went to sit at the back of the court with Karen, while one of the telephonists gave her evidence.

It all got too much for me. Her lies and games were becoming intolerable and I was getting extremely upset and agitated with the whole process. To me it was simple. The evidence and proof that Crackfart had made these calls was laid out bare for all to see. The ladies from the telephone exchange had it all there in writing, so why couldn't she just be found guilty and punished, instead of putting us all through this silly game of hers. The magistrates retired to consider their decision and in the meantime the prosecutor and dad were doing their best to get me to leave the court for the sake of my health. I did eventually leave and it was barely ten minutes before the result was through. Ginny had been detained on a four week court treatment order, which meant she had to go into Fairmile Mental Hospital for assessment and court reports. Sentencing was adjourned until then.

    One month later I returned to the court to see Ginny receive a fine of £100, plus she had to pay £198 in court costs. It was a punishment I suppose, but not one I had really expected. Yet again the previous conditional discharge and the bind over were ignored. I had hoped they would use these in a bid to calm her down for a while. We had all been grateful for the month long respite we had received while Ginny had been in hospital, and as part of her sentence she was to return to Fairmile for a further week's treatment. I finally came to the conclusion and accepted that justice had been done on this occasion.

On her eventual return home, Ginny immediately changed her phone line from British telecom to that of a cable company. No sooner had the engineer left our phone rang. No way, she wouldn't, would she? We laughed. It was indeed Ginny and she proceeded to make a further ten nuisance calls to our home. It looked like nothing had changed and the battle was to go on. I guessed Ginny had realised that by changing phone companies we would have to start all over again with the trace and build a new case, giving her more time to drive us to despair.

She taunted us from her driveway, laughingly thanking us for her months holiday in Fairmile, saying how much she had enjoyed it, how good it had been to be away from us all. Again she found her appearance in court to be very amusing. Just as quickly as she was laughing she switched to her menacing growl mode, "Remember I can play the system. You will not beat me. I will win and I will continue until you are all finished"

Over the months Crackfart was in and out of court for a various array of minor offences, and usually I tried my best to attend. She always played the silly games and always demanded that I be evicted from the public gallery. The result was always the same, and she continually got off with another warning. I was beginning to think she had more lives than a cat. She wasted so much of everyone's time that the magistrates just wanted to deal with her as quickly, quietly and easily as possible.

Throughout the years since I had been in trouble myself, I had stayed in contact with my probation officer. She was my confidant and friend, and during this stressful time with the Jekyll and Hyde Ginny, I had seen a lot more of her. Mrs H. had changed jobs within the probation service and was now working on the Court Divert Team, which dealt with the mental health side of things. I felt it helpful to be able to off load my concerns of old Crackfart to someone who had some understanding of the issues involved. More importantly though she helped me to appreciate what drove Ginny's apparent mindless actions. Mrs H. made me realise that even the times that Ginny appeared sane and well, these actions were still powered by the control of her mental illness.

Some months after the charades of the nuisance call case, Ginny was again hauled up in front of the magistrates on a breach of the peace charge. Mrs H. was aware that I planned to go along as usual, but on the morning of the hearing I received a phone call from her secretary asking me to stay away. This was apparently at the request of Mrs H. It was now that my relationship with her came into question. It had never struck me before that through her job she may come into contact with Ginny.

Selfishly, I felt betrayed and angry. How could she do this to me after all these years, she was supposed to be my friend after all. I wondered why she hadn't told me she was in contact with my arch enemy. Perhaps if she had I wouldn't have felt so uneasy and distrustful of her. We were supposed to be meeting up the next day but the moment I received that phone call, I knew I would never see her again. I felt like something precious had been stolen from me and a deep dark sadness filled my heart. Lots of thoughts were running through my mind. Had she spoken to Ginny about me? Whose side of the story would she believe now? I felt threatened and vulnerable and very bad tempered.

It was an impulsive and childish decision that made me miss our appointment and one I regretted deeply. I decided to write and apologise for not letting her know that I would not be going, and then went on to explain why. By return of post I had a reply from her that immediately settled a lot of the questions that were eating away at me. It turned out that nobody else on the divert team was available to deal with Ginny that day in court, and as it was part of her job she'd had no choice but attend with Ginny. Ginny's case had since been allocated to a colleague and Mrs H. had kept contact to a minimum. It was in her professional opinion that if I were to keep a low profile on the day of Ginny's hearing, then it would make matters a lot easier for us all when she returned home. She also didn't want Ginny to know that we were friends and that was the reason for the phone call, nothing anymore sinister than that. Mrs H. had also had to drive Ginny home, but instead of dropping her outside her house, she had made Ginny get out of the car at the end of the road in a bid to avoid old Crackfart realising we knew each other. We did eventually meet up again and I was reassured to hear that she would never speak to Ginny about me and vice versa. For a little while I still felt uncomfortable with the situation, but I had trusted her for over 12 years and I wasn't going to let Ginny drive a wedge between us. I had to be grown up about it all. It didn't seem to matter what I said, where I went, what I did or who I knew,

Ginny had wormed her way into just about every part of my life. This time however I was not going to allow her to munch the safety net from beneath me.

It is twenty plus years now since I was on probation and my relationship with Mrs H. is still as strong as ever. She is still my confidant and friend.

Chapter Ten

The day of Karen's wedding was fast approaching and there appeared to be no let up in Ginny's behaviour. If anything her persecutions increased, but were aimed more directly at my sister.

"You stupid cow, I know all about you too. Oh yes, three underage abortions"

THUD! Half a house brick landed at our feet as we stood in the back doorway.

"Oi! I'm talking to you! Are you listening? Three underage abortions at just fifteen, now you got AIDS just like your sister, and as for you" she continued pointing at a bemused David, "You should know better than to get involved with that family, you must be barmy. Oh I forgot you're her pimp that's right, you get a share of the takings"

And so it went on, her voice penetrating every area of our lives. Sometimes during these attacks on my sister she would fling a barrage of insults at one or other of us, just to remind us that the rest of the family were not off the hook yet either.

Day after day it continued. "Prostitute prostitute who wants to be with you?"

Enough was enough, Crackfart's voice was reaching fever pitch which usually meant that a physical attack was imminent. But instead of retaliating and bellowing back, Karen simply and calmly went into the shed and after a few bangs and crashes reappeared holding my red bicycle light. Switching it on Karen strode down the path and placed it on the tall brick gate post dividing the two properties.

"Open for business, cheap rates. Open for business, any takers?" she yodelled, while prancing around on the pavement.

Ginny could not believe what she was witnessing and for a few moments she stood, mouth open staring in silence, before once again leaping from foot to foot,

"I knew it, I knew it. Prostitute, you hear everyone, Karen is a prostitute".

It was hysterically funny. While Karen pretended to tout for business, Ginny looked like she was doing an apaches war dance. It wasn't until David and I fell about laughing that Ginny finally cottoned on that we were taking the Mickey. By God, was she infuriated! Dashing indoors she returned a few seconds later armed with a bag of soggy rubbish that consequently ended up splattered about our feet. It was time to retreat.

Obviously Crackfart's enunciations of Karen's so called chosen career were a complete figment of her imagination. Karen was in fact a chef manager who never had and never intended to sell her body to anyone for anything. As for the abortions, well we came to the conclusion that she must have had three immaculate conceptions, followed by three immaculate terminations.

Karen had met David, who was three years older than herself when she was just fifteen and although quite young, their relationship soon grew into something more solid and it was now, some ten years later that they were finally tying the knot. It was the eve of the wedding.

Mum, Dad, and some of the neighbours had gone up to the hall were the reception was to be held to prepare it for the following afternoon. Karen, I and four of her friends stayed behind to enjoy Karen's last night of freedom. The weather was hot, the atmosphere light and we sat about the garden laughing and joking. All was going well until one of us – I don't remember who – mentioned the dreaded Crackfart.

Ginny had not yet returned home from her daily excursion to London, but was due back at any moment. I believe she had been aware of an excited air of increased activity by ourselves, but didn't have a clue as to what was occurring tomorrow. There had been a few incidents that week whereby she had behaved more oddly than usual but we just put that down to changes in her mental illness. She now had a thing about David's little Nissan Micra. She would wander around it when it was parked out front on the road, never touching, but just looking with that glint in her eye. David spent hours lovely keeping it in tip top condition and was convinced she was going to ruin the metallic paint on it. He would watch her out of the window, just in case.

Karen had also run into Crackfart up at the precinct and to avoid confrontation had tried to do a runner. She'd just bought this enormous bean bag and trying to run with it proved difficult. So in a bid not to be recognised she had stuck it on her head. Unfortunately this had had the opposite effect. Not only did she look like a furry overgrown mushroom floundering its way to the car park, the bag she had just purchased had a hole in it. She left a trail of little white polystyrene beans in her wake.

Having laughed ourselves silly over Karen's recent mishap the conversation took on a more serious note. With Ginny due back at any moment we decided we had to get in first and freak her out in the hope she would retreat indoors for the next twenty four hours, and prevent any disharmony on Karen's big day. We had to show the witch that we were not scared of her. It was a bit of a risk but a silly plan had already formed in our minds.

Kazzie, Mooser and Tina were sent out front to watch for Ginny's return. In the meantime Karen, Emma and I settled ourselves down cross legged in a triangle on a huge concrete slab behind dads shed. In the middle of us sat a huge big green plastic blow up frog that Mike had bought me for Christmas. It was in a position that made it look like it was ready to pounce. It had this comical but at the same time, mean looking expression on its face, depending on what angle you looked at in from. Then we waited, and waited until finally the warning came. The other three being petrified of Crackfart scarpered indoors. Mooser hid in the larder, while Kazzie and Tina fled upstairs and crouched beneath the bedroom window.

Ginny's garage was at the end of her back garden and every time she came home she always went down to check on it before going indoors. The moment she drew level with the shed, Emma let out this enormous wail, and with arms straight out in front of her began chanting to the frog. Karen and I followed suit. Within seconds the garden was filled with this hideously painful screeching and wailing. Old Crackfart nearly jumped out of skin. She hadn't seen us statically sat there waiting in silence. For what seemed like eternity, but was probably only a few minutes, she just stood there, open mouthed staring at us, before trying to talk over the din.

"You're mad the lot of you. Mad!"

The wails got louder, Ginny got louder, the wails louder still, Ginny was screaming at us now and we were in our element, we were in control and we were not running away. Suddenly Emma dropped the pitch to a low kind of hum and pointing both her arms and the frog at Ginny began chanting;

"Ye-o-yay-o frog of Mecca! Drive out all the evil spirits, ye-o-yay-o frog of Mecca! Drive out all the evil spirits, from HER!"

The three of us were now chanting in harmony, faster and faster raising the pitch to that painful wailing again, our outstretched arms all pointing in Ginny's direction. Emma's face looked so serious that Karen and I were struggling to hold it together without breaking out in laughter. Finally the witch couldn't stand it any longer and with her hands covering her ears speed off to the safety of her house. Just to be on the safe side Emma carried this charade on for a while longer. I am convinced to this day that Emma hypnotised herself in the process. I can honestly say I've never laughed so much in all my life. The other three now seeing the coast was clear came and joined us in the garden.

Every now and then we would hear Ginny unlocking her back door as if to come out, so either Karen, or myself would chuck a rubber ball at it. It would hit her door then bounce off of her concrete and back over the fence to our waiting hands. At one point Ginny took a risk and flew out to close her big iron gates that were gaping open halfway up her drive. The moment she was back indoors I jumped over the fence and reopened them. Ginny continually kept trying to come out to close them again but the rubber ball kept her at bay. By 10pm all was quiet and it appeared our scare tactics of magical powers had done the trick and so in jubilation we began to sing;

"Hey ho the witch is dead, the wicked witch, the wicked witch, hey ho the witch is dead la-la-la-la-la"

We kept this up for quite a while and over the years this song became our weapon. Every time Ginny began to threaten us either physically or verbally we would sing over the top of her, 'Hey ho the witch is dead – la-la-la-la laaaa!'

We did feel a bit guilty about our actions that night, especially when the police attended, but by then all was quiet. We had picked on Ginny without any clear reason and lowered ourselves to that of her childish behaviour. While we knew what we had done was wrong, it did feel good to be in control for once, while also giving her a taste of her own medicine.

The next morning our house was a hive of activity. The bridesmaids arrived along with the hairdresser and make up lady. The house was noisy and full of laughter, yet Ginny was nowhere to be seen. It was all getting a bit much for me to cope with so I set off to get my hair done by Mandy, a friend who worked in a salon up at the precinct. I had just had my hair washed and was sitting in front of the mirror waiting to have it styled when a reflection caught my eye, then I heard the voice.

I don't know how Ginny knew where I had gone as I had driven up to the shops, but here she was standing at the reception desk demanding to have her hair cut. In a frantically low and mumbled voice I was begging Mandy to take me out the back to avoid any embarrassment. Mandy summonsed the receptionist to the back of the shop and told her to get rid of the lady at the desk and not to ask any questions. Anxious, stressed and shaking, Mandy and I listen as Ginny was told there were no appointments left that day and asked if she would like to come back on Monday. This did not go down very well and Ginny flipped her lid. Screaming and shouting she was telling everyone that she knew I was hiding and began spouting the usual rubbish about me being dangerous and having AIDS. I was almost in tears and thought she would never go, but the lady on reception had threatened to call the police and surprisingly Ginny left. I was so embarrassed and refused to go back out to the front of the salon. It ended up with Mandy doing my hair, with me perched on a little stool out in the back car park.

The wedding went off without a hitch or any intervention from Ginny and we were very surprised and delighted that Karen did not require a police escort down the drive when she left for the church. As it happened we were helped by the neighbours who had turned out on mass to wave and cheer Karen on her way. As they began to gather Ginny had made a hasty retreat indoors obviously realising that she didn't stand a chance against the whole road. Any plans she may have had to spoil the day were dashed, and thankfully it was the last we saw of her for over a week.

Chapter Eleven

The summer time always seemed to tip Ginny that little bit further over the edge. Perhaps because the weather was nice and we all tended to spend a lot more time out in the garden and sunshine, that it irritated her as we would have been in constant view.

She would have been aware of our activities more than usual and anything we did either individually or as a family seemed to send her into a frenzied spin of spiteful retaliation. Crackfart just couldn't bear to see us happy and enjoying ourselves. We didn't put on an act or pretend to be ultra happy, we were just ordinary people trying to live an ordinary everyday life.

Despite everything I still had this deep desire to understand the mechanics of Ginny. I wanted to get inside her head and pick away at the components of her mind, piecing them together like a jigsaw puzzle until a complete and clear picture evolved. If she had been made of meccano I could have unbolted her and put her back together again in good working order. I think I knew I would never understand the workings of her mind or the mental illness she suffered, but I studied her all the same.

During this time new and worrying elements to her illness began to emerge. There were times when she appeared to have very little respect for herself, and then there were the obsessions. One of these obsessions was the sudden and intense interest she had taken in her washing line. I often used to wonder if she was contemplating hanging herself on it. She always had this weird and chilling expression on her face when she was 'playing' with it. It wasn't long before this new obsession turned into a tool to aid her persecutions. It gave Ginny the perfect opportunity to be ear-wigging my family without it seeming obvious that was what she was doing. Very rarely did any washing actually appear on this wondrous green line, but she always seemed to be playing with it. Ginny would go out through her crumbling garden archway and just stand and stare at it, hands on hips. Other times she would jiggle it about making out it was wobbling in its stand and then spin it around and around wiping its spider web formation over and over again, even if it was dry. It would continue on and off at various times of the day, day in day out. If any of us unknowingly ventured outside during her obsessive ritual we would certainly know it. All manner of the usual missiles would come hurtling from behind the garden wall. It was like an angry reaction to us, like we were intruding and interrupting her ritualistic cravings.

  I think one of the worst things Ginny did to us all over the years was her knack of continually popping up like a jack in the box and screeching abuse at such high pitch, that it literally scared you half to death and sent you pulse rocketing through the roof. Although this wasn't a physical threat to our lives, her evil cackle would be expressed in such a way that you did actually wonder if you were in danger. These threats were now made in such a way that you could almost feel the venomous poison spewing from her mouth as her mottled face contorted with rage. Ginny's screwed up eyes blazed bolts of electricity in every direction. They were like a spark to tinder shrub land desperate to make contact in order to mature into massive flames, in a bid to destroy every living thing around them. Some days we could ignore her threats other days they felt so real.

  I had just about had enough of Ginny's heart stopping episodes and in a moment of complete madness I cleared the fence in one giant leap. I began hacking away at her washing line with a pair of scissors I had subconsciously grabbed from the kitchen. Now with my weapon in motion every chop brought with it a huge sense of relief and a gratifying feeling of being so powerful and clever. Having shredded her line in seconds and rendering it useless, I turned on my heel and in a calm, slow deliberate manner climbed back over the fence. I replaced the scissors to their respected place in the cutlery drawer and joined Mum in the lounge to watch television. It was like the last few moments hadn't happened. Mum would most certainly have had forty fits had she been aware of what I had just done, and I just seemed to erase it from my mind. There wasn't a peep out of Crackfart so I guessed she had missed my moment of power raising glory.

As old Crackfart regularly reported me to the police for crimes I hadn't committed, I was not unduly worried about the consequences. Therefore it came as no surprise to me to very next day when the inspector phoned asking that I attend an interview regarding criminal damage to Ginny's property.

The interview was set for four days time and during this period I pondered over my actions. It was such a petty crime but one that could land me in court because of my misspent youth. The day before I was due at the police station I decided to replace the broken line. I waited until Crackfart went out and having already purchased a new line told Mum what I had previously done. I spent the best part of an hour trying to rethread the blasted thing and it was no easy challenge. Not only was I struggling with the design, I had Mum chomping away in my ear telling me to get out of Crackfart's garden. I did finally manage to complete my task and the next day went along to the police interview feeling a little less guilty.

During the actual police interview I never once admitted or denied causing damage to the line. I was very careful how I worded my answers, usually answering a question with a question, responses like, "Do you really think I'd resort to such petty measures" and "the line looked fine this morning when I left home, have you inspected it?"

However once the tape was off and I was safely on my way out, I did admit to losing my rag and causing the damage. It was a big risk but I felt better for being honest, eventually. As I had replaced the line it was agreed to let the matter drop. All in all my actions hadn't achieved much in the long term, but had satisfied a short term need, and probably stopped me from doing something far worse. It did cause a lot of stress but we did get five days of totally undisturbed peace and quiet.

The months passed and nothing changed. The police came and went and I went and returned from interviews at the police station. The threats continued sometimes causing physical harm to one neighbour or another or me. The greatest harm Ginny was causing was to my mental stability. I often contemplated my worth and place in society, my physical health also began to deteriorate as a result of the long standing and unresolved issues. I was still being passed from pillar to post by the local authorities and the mental health service. By now this had all affected me so badly I was myself under the care of the community mental health team. In one respect this was at times helpful, but at other times very frustrating as my Social Worker was unwilling to work through the issues Ginny had and was continuing to raise within me. My own G.P. Was however very supportive and could quite clearly see the change in me. He felt the continued harassment of both Ginny and the police was having a detrimental effect and arranged to have a meeting with myself and the inspector at his surgery. Needless to say the inspector never turned up neither did he ring to say he wouldn't be attending. This happened on two occasions and I believe Doc G. had a conversation with him over the phone instead. It did help for a while as the police seemed to leave me alone for a bit and didn't always take old Crackfart's allegations so seriously. Ginny had also been a patient at the same surgery as myself, so the G.P. was able to explain a bit more fully the state of her mental health.

    Crackfart soon realised that her actions were now having less effect on all parties concerned and began to make anonymous calls to my doctor out of hours. She kept claiming I was acting violently and irrationally and needed sectioning for everyone's safety. I would be watching telly in the evenings and Doc G. would call to ask if everything was ok with me. It was always the same. He knew it was Ginny calling him but he checked me out just to cover his back. He was so apologetic and in the end it became a bit of a joke between us.

    Ginny was becoming increasingly frustrated that after three years she still had not broken us, especially myself and began to resort to more desperate measures. There were the usual invitations for us to go over to her place and fight her. It was so hard being restrained. I think if I had of taken her up on her offer I would have lost total control because of the pent up anger inside of me. Three years is a long time to be physically and mentally abused. Karen was best at handling these fiery situations and Ginny would scream "C'mon you fat cow, come over and fight me, show me what you're made of" and Karen would reply "Don't you know, moo, fat cows, moo, can't jump over fences, moo!" Although she was hurt and angry by Ginny's words, Karen always managed to break the tension and make us laugh.

After another brief interlude of peace I went out one morning to find my car had been 'keyed' right along the back wing. I was mortified. I had not witnessed Ginny doing this but I could tell by her taunting words of delight that she was the culprit. Ginny had always been so careful not to be seen by others when she made her attacks, only now she didn't seem to care.

'Fancy Dan' who live in the next street, who we believed was her boyfriend, but found out later was actually her father, had witnessed her behaviour first hand. Despite this he was continually telling us to back off and leave her alone. Apparently we were big bullies. He always stuck up for the evil witch regardless of whether the police were involved or not. She committed all manner of criminal offences in front of him, yet he made no obvious attempt to stop her. Maybe he was just as frightened of her as we all were. Watching the way he behaved on occasions made us wonder if he was as batty as she was. We really did need that independent witness and prayed it wouldn't be long before Ginny slipped up.

Weeks went by and the summer was drawing to a close. We hoped Ginny would go into hibernation like a tortoise, but it wasn't to be.

Late on in the August of that year, I bumped into PC Granddad up at the precinct and he informed me Ginny had made more serious allegations against me, whereby I had stolen money from her purse. There was nothing unusual about this and I laughed it off. It was only when he went on to say that she had also reported me for stealing her underwear from her washing line and continually exposing myself to her from my landing window, did my blood run cold. A prickly heat swept down my back and made my face glow red. I certainly wasn't guilty of any of these allegations but her perverted claims had embarrassed me. The only explanation I could come up with was if I had crossed the landing to my bedroom after taking a shower and the landing light had been on. If she had been spying on us as she usually did, then of course she would have copped an eyeful. Standing there in the precinct I suddenly felt very panicky and vulnerable. Although she was nowhere in sight it felt like her eyes were boring into me and it made my skin crawl to think of her watching me. Nervously I tried to laugh it off with the police officer but I was already imagining the questioning that lay ahead of me at the police station.

It was not until November that these allegations came to the fore, and I had until then, managed to erase the previous conversation from my mind. During the interview it was stated that Crackfart had reported the allegations of occurring on and after the 25th of September. How therefore had P.C. Granddad known about them way back in August? Nobody seemed able to piece it all together and find an answer to my question, and so once again the whole thing was written off, but not before I had been put through the ringer. It was put down to a figment of Ginny's over active imagination. Yet again she got away with it and yet again she had caused me great suffering.

I knew Ginny was mentally ill and maybe I should've been more understanding, making allowances for that fact, but I just couldn't, not anymore. There were times when she was so convincingly sane that you couldn't look at her as anything but evil. Nobody really knew what she was doing to me, not fully. My tolerance levels were at an all time low and along with my weight my self esteem had again plummeted. I spent the majority of my time feeling stressed and angry, not only at her, but the whole of society for not sitting up and listening.

One question turned over and over in my mind. Why was Ginny allowed to behave the way she was doing and get away with it, and also still be allowed to live within the community when she was obviously so ill and unstable and worse still, dangerous. It made my blood boil. Hundreds of hours must have been spent on her wasting police time, yet she was never charged with this. What would have to happen before any real seriousness would be given to this whole charade of hers? If charades was what Ginny wanted to play, then charades it would be. I too could play mind games and proving to her that she was not the master at it gave me the will to carry on.

I discovered by accident one afternoon that Ginny did not like having the bible quoted at her. While she ranted at me I quietly, but purposefully began reading it aloud in a bid to block out her tedious voice. She had no choice other than to listen to me or go back indoors if she didn't like it. Amid flying pebbles and smelly rubbish I read anything and everything. I quoted passages from the death of Jesus, to Revelations, from Psalms to Proverbs and even Job. I didn't choose these passages deliberately, it was just a random act of how I opened and turned the pages of the bible. Ginny's reaction surprised me. For once she actually looked terrified and just stood there with her hands covering her ears, screeching at me to stop. Realising I was on to something here I continued to read forcefully on, raising and changing the tone of my voice to add meaning and emphasis to the passage in hand. Knowing it was freaking her out made me feel powerful and safe. The mighty word of the Lord often won through and rescued me during many occasions of her ranting.

There were other little acts, some of childish stupidity that got me through those depressing years of torture. One night Jo and I had stopped at the chippie on our way home from the sports club and had parked the car in front of the estate agents. While we sat there munching on our chips we spotted a huge pile of 'For Sale' signs along the side of the building. Wouldn't it be great if one of them appeared in Ginny's garden I had mused to Jo. If only she would move away I could get my life back. We looked at each other and laughed.

As soon as we had finished our chips I reversed the car down the side of the building and opened the boot. The signs all seemed to be on six or seven foot posts and only having a little fiesta we struggled to get one in the boot. The post came right through the front seats between Jo and me, while the sign hung out of the back of the boot. What the heck it was dark, nobody would see and so we set off towards home with the view to planting it in Ginny's front garden.

We must have driven up and down the road at least ten times with the sign happily waving to the world from the boot of the car, before we got the courage to carry out our plan. Parking a few houses up from Ginny's, we hopped out and quickly pulled the sign from the boot and flung it to the ground. Crawling along the pavement in front of Crackfart's house I was filled with mixed emotions. While on one hand I was petrified the old bag would spot us and launch a counter attack I couldn't help but get a fit of the giggles. It was a silly thing we were doing and probably wouldn't achieve much other than to wind Ginny up, but there was no going back now. My heart was pounding as I went along on my hands and knees; it was a similar feeling to that of getting caught bunking off or smoking at school as a teenager. I poked my head up above the garden wall and grabbing the sign off of Jo I hurtled it up and over, stabbing its stake viciously into the soft earth in Crackfart's border. It felt so very satisfying.

I hardly dared look out of the window the next morning, but when Mum came running into my room saying "Look, look out of the window, there's a For Sale sign in Ginny's garden."

I had no choice but to stare out at my handy work. I had shoved the post into the ground with such haste the night before that it was leaning to one side at an angle with the actual sign dangling over Ginny's garden wall and sticking out onto the pavement. What a sorry job I had done.

"Let's hope she is on the move soon and leaves us in peace," Mum continued. "I really don't think I can take much more of her. Wouldn't it be wonderful if she left?"

I felt guilty, ever so guilty for getting mums hopes up. I had always justified my retaliation to Ginny's behaviour as that of self defence of my sanity. That day however I learnt a valuable lesson. What is funny and a coping mechanism for one could actually have an adverse effect on another. How disappointed Mum would be if she knew it was me having a joke.

To some people reading this it probably doesn't sound that much of a big deal. What's a bit of verbal and a few missiles between neighbours? But it was more than that. Living the reality day after day and coping with the emotional and mental torment it brings with it, has to take its toll eventually. Ginny was devouring our lives. Slowly bit by bit she was tearing us apart, both individually and as a family. The disharmony within the family was deepening and leaving an unspoken fear.

During the three years or so we had been under attack from old Crackfart mum had suffered a couple of strokes. Her blood pressure was permanently and dangerously high and the doctors at the hospital were having trouble getting it under control, which was in turn was making her vulnerable to further strokes. While we appreciate it is not Ginny's fault that Mum had this illness, we believe she certainly played a major role in triggering and maintaining it through her wicked behaviour.

Just before the first stroke occurred Mum had received a letter from the Mental Health Service, inviting her to go and view the records they had on file about her. As Ginny had taken our surname it was obviously a reply to a request she herself had made in the hope of digging some dirt on Mum, by pretending to be her. We'd had the same postman for years and I assume he thought the house number on the envelope had been mistyped, and so put it through our letterbox. Mum responded to the invitation:

> *Thank you for your letter advising when I can come and view my records. I can confirm that this time is convenient for me.*
>
> *How I come to have records of my personal life in your files is a mystery to me, and came as a complete shock when I opened your letter. Part of the mystery can perhaps be answered by the fact that the person living next door, known to us as MRS GINNY CRACKFART, has obviously informed you that she wishes to be known as Mrs O' Down. In a recent incident which involved her being in police custody, she signed a statement using my name.*
>
> *This is yet further evidence of a provocative nature to be added to the catalogue of events of the past few years. It would seem you condone such behaviour from a person of alleged mental instability.*
>
> *I await you reply with interest.*

Mum was quite willing to attend the arranged meeting as it would provide a good opportunity to have a face to face discussion regarding our concerns about Ginny, and the harassment we were suffering.

Apart from that very first phone call, the Mental Health Service had refused to acknowledge ours or Ginny's existence. They would not return calls, ignored letters we wrote to them, or told us they had passed them on somewhere else but they must have got lost in the post. When I asked for support for myself I was initially turned away. Even using a hypothetical conversation they point blank refused to talk to me. When I was eventually assessed and allocated a social worker, there was still a reluctance to let me express how deeply this was affecting me, and to date I have never really been given the opportunity to do so.

While I understand agree there should be rules of patient confidentiality, I believe these were taken to unwritten extremes and as a human being with feelings I was treated appallingly. They could at least have allowed me to talk through how Ginny's actions were affecting me without disclosing any personal information about Ginny to me. I am glad to say that this service has greatly improved over the last ten to fifteen years.

We received an almost immediate response to mums letter.

I do apologise for the fact this letter seems to have come to you by mistake. We do not hold any information concerning you here. There is no point you visiting the office as there is no information to see.

Once again I apologise for any distress which receipt of this letter caused.

That was the last we heard about the matter and in fact the last we ever heard from them. Unfortunately though not the last we heard from old Crackfart. Her plans to find out about Mum and her continual failings of false allegations and harassment against us, coupled with the fact she was making a fool of herself, didn't deter her in any way. If anything it had the opposite effect, passionately driving her on to find other ways to impose herself on everyone, particularly myself.

Chapter Twelve

Ginny wasn't travelling to London anymore and I was no longer working. Physically my health had improved a little, but mentally I was going downhill fast. The only thing that was keeping me alive at the moment in time was rambling. Not in the verbal sense but physically, walking.

Day after day come rain or shine I escaped the intolerable suffocating abuse of Ginny by traipsing through the countryside. I came to love the sights and sounds of nature, the damp earthy smell that rose from the lightly dusted ground as I walked through the woods. Flowers scented by the sun, their bobbing heads smiling and blowing in the breeze. I'd listen to the hum of a far off tractor and the trill trilling of the birds coming together in harmony as I plodded on. I'd often cry tears of freedom. It was a different world where I didn't have to protect myself or my family. Even as I write this, I'm back there, back by the quarry in Knowle Hill kicking the dusty leaves, staring up through the leafy green sunlit gaps of the tree tops, reaching for the freedom of my strangulated life.

I didn't often tell my parents when Crackfart's missiles had scored a hit on my tired and tense body. If they were about at the time obviously they saw or heard the goings on, but it seemed pointless us all getting angry and upset. It just wasn't worth it. Keeping this to myself was extremely difficult and it ate away at me. I felt like I was being naughty. Not telling was keeping secrets from my family. It was causing a pressure to build within me and one more incident might just set an explosion firing off in all directions.

That incident was to come sooner rather than later. Crackfart continually chipped away at me with verbal digs and the odd rock or two, but nothing really major. It was now the middle of January 1996 and I had been medically retired from the civil service. I had been diagnosed with severe bilateral Menieres Disease, coupled with stress, anxiety and depression. This meant I got a monthly pension and a one off lump sum on my retirement. My big cheque had finally arrived and I set off happy as a millionaire to deposit it into my savings account. I wasn't really paying much attention to my surroundings, probably too busy day dreaming about what I could do with three and a half thousand pounds, to notice who was going in and out of the bank. I pushed open the door and there stood Ginny staring right back at me. I tried to get out as quickly as I could but it was too late.

"That's her, that's the one. She stole my money from my account, stop her, arrest her, she's a mental criminal, a thief".

My legs turned to jelly and I began to shake all over, I felt hot and cold all at the same time and really thought I was going to be sick. I just stood there as everyone turned to stare at me. Ginny flew across the few steps between us and grabbed hold of my right arm. Her grip was like an incredibly vice as she threw my wobbly little body across the floor and slammed me into the wall.

"This is her, the one that took three and a half thousand pounds out of my account. You must do something, NOW" she screamed.

Oh flipping heck, not again I thought to myself, she's in psychic spook mode. How did she know the exact amount that was on the cheque that I was just about to deposit? This had happened so often it had me convinced she really did have our house bugged.

Crackfart's weight bearing through her arms forced me harder into the wall. So much so it felt like the bones in my spine were being crushed. I was pinned down and terrified. A voice kept rolling around my head telling me not to fight back, if you fight back you'll be arrested, don't fight back, don't retaliate and don't hurt her.

I began yelling at the bank staff to call the police. Some of the customers hurriedly left while others shrunk back from the wild and sweating Ginny. She had not lessened her grip on me and the cashiers sat rooted to their seats and I began to cry. Not one person came to my aid.

"Get off me, I sobbed, I haven't done anything wrong. This lady is a paranoid Schizophrenic and is well known to the police, please call the police".

Still nobody moved. I was angry now and very embarrassed. There was an intensifying pain in the top of my arm distracting me from protecting myself. Ginny was screaming a mixture of lies and abuse, her head continually turning from me to the counter clerk. Her mouth was so close to my face that I could feel little droplets of her saliva hit me as she spat out her words. It was claustrophobic and I was becoming more panicky by the second. Suddenly a surge of adrenalin ripped through my body releasing a natural instinct to defend myself. Yet the more I struggled, the louder and more aggressive Ginny became.

"You're my hostage, you're my hostage, you're not going anywhere you thief"

She was absolutely hysterical as I wiggled and kicked my way towards the door. Ginny was flinging me about like a limp rag doll in the jaws of an angry dog. Finally I struggled free from my jacket and left her standing there, holding it open mouthed.

I felt terrible as I ran from the bank. Somehow I managed to find my way to the Doctors surgery some one hundred yards away and arrived at the desk unable to talk any sense. As the receptionist couldn't understand me and the doctor had a patient with him, she guided me though to the treatment room. It took the nurse some time to calm me down and when I was finally able to string a few words together explaining the last six or seven minutes, she immediately handed me the phone to call the police.

I felt sick, faint and extremely weak and was probably suffering from shock. Looking at my arm I found a huge purple bruise, the size of an orange with little ones dotted all around it where her steel like fingers had gripped me.

I dialled 999 and in a feeble voice requested the police come to my assistance as I had just been assaulted and the offender was probably still lurking around the shops. I was told a patrol car was on its way. As the conversation continued however and I was asked my name and if I knew the name of my assailant, the operators attitude changed. The moment I gave my surname followed by Mrs Ginny Crackfart, he didn't want to know.

"Oh, we don't have a patrol available at the moment, go and report the incident at your local police station"

"But I need to collect my jacket from the bank it has my cheque, money and other personal items in it. She might attack me again so I can't go in there alone"

"Woodley station know all about the ongoing conflict between you, let them deal with it. Thank You". And the call was ended.

I was angry at having the crime against me belittled. Why did nobody take this situation seriously, it was so unfair. I stormed out of the surgery miraculously recovered from my earlier shock and marched over to the bank. I was ready to go to war against Ginny but she had gone and I found myself somewhat disappointed. I found my jacket, paid in my cheque and asked the cashiers if they would be willing to give a statement to the police on my behalf. Both ladies were willing and at last I had the independent witnesses needed to get old Crackfart prosecuted.

The earlier conversation with the police operator had now taken my attention and it took only seconds for my optimism to evaporate. Anger once again reared within me and I stormed off to the car park like a power walker going for gold. With gears crunching in temper I headed straight for Woodley police station.

My complaint was acknowledged, a statement taken and reassurances given that officers would contact the cashiers. I was to hear from them in due course. Huh! That usually meant that the issue of no great importance and they would drag their heels in getting Ginny to court. I'd heard it all before and left for home feeling dejected, rather weary and extremely angry. The day's events and ever changing emotions had suddenly caught up with me and all I wanted to do was to have a hot shower and snuggle down into the safe comfort of my bed.

By the next morning I felt recovered enough to go and have my bruises photographed for evidence. As the police would not do this I had to get them done at my own expense, with the risk that because I had, they may not be able to be used in court. It was a lot of aggravation for possibly a negative outcome.

Upon my return from the studio Ginny kicked off again saying she was going to have me arrested. I took no notice of her verbal wittering and went indoors to get some peace. Within minutes two police cars came tearing up the road with sirens blaring. This time she had reported me for apparently waving a gun in her face. Once again all hell broke loose as I tried to defend my innocence.

I think what really got my goat was the fact Ginny would make silly time wasting accusations against me and have officers running about after her like she was some wonderful God to be worshipped. Yet when I am physically assaulted I receive little or no support and any I do receive I have to fight tooth and nail to get.

Later that day I wrote to the inspector of Woodley police expressing my concerns at the inequality of service given to both the fore mentioned incidents. It appeared more attention had again been paid to a compulsive liar with a history of mental illness, rather than me, the victim. I did receive a response from him by return of post.

> *The fact two cars attended at Mrs Crackfart's request was due to the nature of her call and the grading it was given by the officers in the control room, who perhaps, individually had never met her before.*

> *We do attempt on every occasion to deal with both parties in a wholly unbiased way and will continue to do so.*

What a load of tosh, Unbiased? I think not. The true fact of the matter is that a person suffering known mental health problems is always given priority and protection regardless of whether they are the victim or the instigator. Whereas there is nothing set in place to protect the victims from the crimes of the mentally ill. It is all left in the lap of the Gods, unless the perpetrator, the mentally ill person requests medical intervention, you are basically left to suffer the consequences. The letter went on:

Action is certainly being taken regarding the assault on you by Mrs Crackfart but the offence which was committed does not carry with it a power of arrest for the police. We are dependent on individuals voluntarily attending police stations in order to be interviewed. Mrs Crackfart has so far failed to do this. In this event we will apply for an issue of summons for this interview.

After reading this I was so angry. I realised that all those times the police had rang me telling I had to attend the police station for interview following Ginny's allegations, I could have in fact refused, or least attended as and when I'd felt ready, saving myself the stress and anxiety these situations had caused me. I was relieved however to hear that Ginny was going to be prosecuted for her attack on me and went up the social club to celebrate. It took three months for the case to be heard at the magistrate's court and when it was, it was not what I had expected.

Ginny had of course decided to plead not guilty and I expect this was part of her grand plan to confuse proceedings again. So on the day of the hearing both of the cashiers and myself were called to attend to give evidence. Despite being nervous I was actually looking forward to be having the chance of telling it like it was. This was going to be my moment and I was certainly going to make the most of it.

We were shuffled off to the witness room to be hidden away from Ginny. It was a decision that was made to make life easier for all concerned. Personally I would have like to have sat opposite the old bag in the waiting room, un-nerving her to the point of setting off another attack. Being stuck in this tiny room meant we had no chance of this happening, yet despite not being able to see her, we could still hear all the commotion she was causing to the court usher.

The prosecutor popped along and had a word with me. Her intentions were to apply for Ginny to be put on yet another bind over to keep the peace. This didn't sit well with me at all. What had happened in the bank that day wasn't just a bit of noisy verbal but a physical attack, and I felt a bind over was inappropriate.

"No way, you're having a laugh, I replied. She is already on two bind over's and a conditional discharge and they have had no effect what so ever. Surely these should be acted upon now too. I want her both helped but properly punished at the same time"

"Ok, I've noted your comments" she replied.

We waited patiently for over two hours, chatting amongst ourselves and putting the world to rights. It was stifling hot and I began to pace around to stretch my legs and wandered over to the open door. As I leant against the wall I peered out at the milling crowds waiting for cases to be called and to my horror saw Ginny emerge from court number two. That's funny I thought to myself, I hadn't heard her name called out over the tannoy, summoning her to the courtroom. She was grinning from ear to ear as she headed out of the exit in a relaxed, confident and swaggering manner. I bolted down to the reception desk and demanded to know what was happening. I was told to go and wait in the witness room.

Another half an hour passed before the prosecutor arrived to inform us that we were no longer needed. The case had been heard and it was felt a bind-over would suffice on this occasion.

"After all it was only a tug of the arm" the prosecutor said.

"A tug of the arm?" I screamed. "Did you not read our statements and study the photos of the bruises she caused to me? This is ridiculous, do I have to die before the justice system sits up and protects the public. It's a flipping farce!"

The prosecutor lady tried reasoning with me but I wasn't having a bar of it. The case had apparently lasted all of ten minutes. I didn't feel this was long enough to have all the facts heard and I told her I would be reporting her and the magistrates to the crown prosecution service for professional misconduct.

At that moment in time Ginny should have been either in the custody of the authorities or sectioned under the mental health act and locked up in Fairmile Mental Hospital. Instead she was probably enjoying a nice cup of coffee and some lunch in a cafe while laughing her socks off. She had just breached two bind over's and a conditional discharge that had been made in the last twelve months and got away with it. What offender wouldn't be laughing? A miscarriage of justice had just occurred.

I felt I was on the edge of a breakdown. The build up and stress of the case, the persistent aggravation, the continued fear and sleepless nights, coupled with the emotional ups and downs, the hopes and disappointments had finally finished me off. I did write to the crown prosecution service but they simply said the outcome had been the best solution for all concerned and the case was now closed. So much for the British justice system, I thought. There wasn't an ounce of fight left in me, or a smidgen of room for anger. I was physically and mentally exhausted. I really didn't care anymore if she killed me, the sooner she did the sooner this pain and suffering would be over. I was defeated.

That night I was raped by a stranger, who held me against my will for over two hours in my own home. My experiences in court with Ginny Crackfart influenced my decision to drop the charges against this man, which is something I have lived to regret. Maundy Thursday is certainly not a day that I will ever forget.

Epilogue

Since the assault in the bank, I had been struggling to contain myself emotionally. I was now seeing my mental health social worker virtually every week. I often had suicidal thoughts and little self esteem, and there were occasions when I took to self harming in a bid to rid myself of the bad and negative feelings within me, especially since the rape.

    I do not blame Ginny for the problems I was suffering as there were some long standing issues from my past that had really never been dealt with. However, I do believe that Ginny's behaviour played a major role in triggering these off, worsening my condition, especially the menieres attacks, and bringing my inadequacies to the surface.

    For months the threats old Crackfart had made to me felt so real and I truly believed she meant to carry out her plan to kill me. She had now begun to tell me that I was a paranoid evil witch that needed burning on the stake. I took this as just more of her verbal nonsense until one evening she flew down the drive carrying an old pot that she was carefully trying to hold upright. The next I knew she had swung the pot in my direction and the liquid inside it was now winging its way towards me. I managed to dodge most of it but some had splashed around my feet. It had a familiar smell but I couldn't work out what it was. Ginny stood there cackling and laughing. A few days later I was alone at home and had gone out to get something from my car. As I returned along the side of the house Ginny once again tried to douse me in the strange liquid from her old pot. This time the smell was distinct, it was petrol. Again most of it had missed me and as I stood looking down at the bit that had splashed my jeans, Ginny suddenly came towards the fence waving a box of matches in my direction. She was screeching that this was it, it my time to die. I was going to be burnt on the stake. I looked at her in horror as she took a match from the box and struck it on the flint. I wasn't sure if she was actually going to throw it at me or if she was just trying to scare the living daylights out of me, but I wasn't going to hang around to find out. I ran to my car and drove away with no intention of coming back for a long time, if at all.

Because of this threat and the deterioration of my health the police, my GP and my social worker contacted the council in the hope that they could re-house me. It was felt that by my moving out, it would not only keep me safe and give my health a chance, but also possibly resolve the conflict between us. If I was taken out of the equation then Crackfart would not have me to reflect herself into, therefore it might help her settle down as well. I was granted a medical 'A' priority and at the end of February 1996 I was offered a flat to rent in Wokingham.

It was both an exciting and scary time for me. I felt smug that Ginny was unaware of my imminent move and the huge favour she had unknowingly done me. I would never have been able to afford a mortgage, nor would I have been housed for many years under normal circumstances. I didn't move in immediately as the place was in an appalling condition. Every wall was covered in mustard coloured woodchip that was stained with the smell of stale old tobacco smoke. The central heating didn't work either, so I spent the next three weeks travelling between home and the flat.

It was good to get away from Ginny for sixteen hours a day and believe me stripping wallpaper while dancing to the radio with Jo made a refreshing change. I was distracted, having fun and my spirits were lifting.

During my nights back home I was still getting grief from old Crackfart. She made several more allegations against me of theft and assault, while still threatening to kill me, and most nights kept me awake with her ranting. Knowing I would soon be leaving my home of the last thirty years was sad, but at least it gave the strength to carry on. I was not going to let the old bag wind me up anymore, and so I ignored her the best

I could.

Ginny got increasingly frustrated because she didn't know where I was going every day and in a bid to find out even tried befriending me between bouts of abuse. I would smile at her and comment what a lovely day it was as I walked on by. Desperate to draw me back into her world she tried reporting Dad, accusing him of assault, saying she had witnesses. Of course this was just another attempt of her trying to regain control and obviously no witnesses were found because there weren't any. Again it was all a figment of her imagination. Even the police didn't believe it. It did draw a bit of anger from me but I refrained from retaliating.

Not long after I moved into the flat Jo rang me in a terrible state saying Ginny had carried out her threat to report her to Social Services for neglecting her boys. It was so wrong; you wouldn't find a well adjusted, well fed, clean and happy pair of boys anywhere in the world. Social Services had turned up on her doorstep demanding the boys go to their offices for assessment. Understandably so, Jo's partner had flown into a terrible rage and had stormed round to Ginny's. He was mighty angry and began banging his fists on Ginny's front door in a bid to get her to come out. I think it was Mum who persuaded him to leave before Ginny dialled 999 and have him arrested. It was all eventually sorted out with the help from the police but it should never have happened.

Knowing me, or my family meant being targeted by Ginny and had Jo not had the courage to continue to visit mum after I had left home, then none of this would have happened. I was so, so angry.

Later that night me and one of my new neighbours went to the railway line at Twyford and grabbed a couple of rocks. They were those large, roughly shaped pale grey ones that lined the tracks. I drove over to Woodley and parked in the road next to mums. We grabbed a rock each and calmly walked down the alley and along the road to the front of Ginny's house. On the count of three we hurled our rocks at Ginny's windows. My mate aimed for the bottom and I the top. My heart was beating so wildly that I thought it was going to explode out of my chest. There was a seconds silence as we stood there, followed by an almighty crash.

Adrenalin kicked in and we ran off in different direction. My legs felt heavy and dead and I was struggling to run both from the fear, and the fact that I was laughing so much. I didn't care that I had just committed a premeditated offence; I didn't even care if I got arrested, I had gained so much satisfaction from my actions. I needed Crackfart to feel frightened, to be shocked and terrified like she had made so many of us feel over the years. I did admit my crime to the police when questioned about it, but as it was really my first serious offence against Ginny, I got away with a police caution.

As the years went on I spent less and less time at mums. If Ginny did see me visiting she would shout loud enough for people in the next street to hear. She would demand I do jobs for her like clean her windows. I was no longer afraid of her so if she asked I was more than happy to oblige and would make moves to enter her property. She then immediately start screaming Louise O' Down get off of my property, or, Help, Louise O' Down is trying to kill me. There were also many occasions where if she saw me driving along the road she would jump out in front of car forcing me to emergency brake at the very last second. How I never ran her over is a miracle. Of course she would report this to the police saying it was an attempt by me on her life. She even did this when she was with Fancy Dan, and he would come over to the car window and have a go at me, telling me to leave her alone. She also started again with the threats to burn me at the stake, only this time other people saw and heard her and she was eventually taken away, either to court or the mental hospital.

On her return and my not being around much her focus turned to that of the neighbours. She began stalking Jo at the nursery, kicking peoples' dogs, assaulting them or accusing them of her assaulting her. On one occasion she even made a hoax call to the fire brigade saying her house had been set on fire. The nuisance phone calls resumed both to mum and dad's and to other neighbours. On one she said "This is your answer machine, master Message from Reading police station, RETURN TO YOUR PEN!"

Neighbours began to empathise with us. Everything she had done to my family over the last five years, she now did to anyone and everyone for the next three.

Ginny Crackfart was clearly very mentally ill. Perhaps she was unaware of the distress she was causing the neighbourhood. Maybe she was just plain evil and used her illness as a cover, or perhaps it was a mixture of the two. Whatever, people were very afraid of her. Jo's eldest son was so terrified that he used to lock the door behind him when he went in to visit Mum. He was just four years of age!

There isn't really a dramatic ending to my story. Ginny simply vanished. In the May of 1999 a removal van arrived and began loading up Ginny's belongings. The driver told us that Ginny had moved to Middlesex. There have been a couple of sightings of her when we assume she had been visiting her Dad, But I haven't seen her. I don't know how I would respond if I did. Even now thoughts of events of those terrible years provoke a deep fear and anger within me, so I probably wouldn't be responsible for my actions.

Even though Ginny was many miles away and our lives were once again peaceful, she didn't forget us. Some ten years after her move to Middlesex dad received a small parcel in the post from her. Her father had obviously died and contained in the envelope were the keys to his house and other important and official documents. We have no idea why she would want to send these to us. Maybe the loss of her father had triggered her illness again, maybe she wanted to accuse us of theft, or perhaps she thought we were stupid enough to go and enter his house, whereby she could then have us arrested. Who knows? Luckily there was the name of a local solicitor contained within the documents. Dad rang them demanding they come and sign for the package and take it away, which thankfully they did immediately.

I have never experienced another so obnoxious, cruel, nasty and frightening person like Ginny Crackfart in my entire life, and I hope I never have to!

THE END

www.ingramcontent.com/pod-product-compliance
Lightning Source LLC
Chambersburg PA
CBHW071305040426
42444CB00009B/1872